Eric Ambler

Twayne's English Authors Series

Kinley Roby, Editor

Northeastern University

TEAS 507

ERIC AMBLER.
Photograph by Jerry Bauer.

Eric Ambler

Ronald J. Ambrosetti

SUNY College at Fredonia

Twayne Publishers • New York
Maxwell Macmillan Canada • Toronto
Maxwell Macmillan International • New York Oxford Singapore Sydney

Eric Ambler
Ronald J. Ambrosetti

Twayne Publishers
Macmillan Publishing Company
866 Third Avenue
New York, New York 10022

Maxwell Macmillan Canada, Inc.
1200 Eglinton Avenue East
Suite 200
Don Mills, Ontario M3C 3N1

Library of Congress Cataloging-in-Publication Data

Ambrosetti, Ronald J.
Eric Ambler / Ronald J. Ambrosetti.
p. cm.—(Twayne's English authors series; TEAS 507)
Includes bibliographical references and index.
ISBN 0-8057-8369-5
1. Ambler, Eric, 1909– —Criticism and interpretations. 2. Spy stories, English—History and criticism. I. Title. II. Series.
PR6001.M48Z53 1994
823'.912—dc20 94-7612
CIP

The paper used in this publication meets the minimum requirements of American National Standard for Information Sciences—Permanence of Paper for Printed Library Materials, ANSI Z39.48-1984.

10 9 8 7 6 5 4 3 2 1

Printed in the United States of America.

To Ray B. Browne
teacher, friend, and egalitarian

Contents

Preface

In sorting out literary bequests and historical influences in the critical tasks of identifying canon formation and genre constituency, popular literature has traditionally been viewed as a mishmash of formulas, pulp sensations, and sometimes-gifted hucksterism. In the case of Eric Ambler, the static and timeworn classifications of historical criticism must surrender a parochial point of view (Ambler as "father of the spy novel") to a larger, more encompassing critique; such a critique would include Ambler's role in both laying the groundwork for a particular genre of popular literature and shaping the methods and materials of what is increasingly referred to as modern global culture. In short, Eric Ambler is as much responsible for the 1981 best-seller *The White Hotel,* by D. M. Thomas, and a host of other variegated popular novels as he is for the single-handed creation of the modern spy novel. Popular culture, and in particular popular literature, took a peculiar turn in the proletarian 1930s. Because of either the dire necessities forced by a global depression or the tantalizing vision of collectivist hope and aspiration, Anglo-American culture voraciously digested the intellectual legacies of Charles Darwin, Sigmund Freud, and Karl Marx from the nineteenth century. The ingestion of these profound ideas by an eager reading audience in the decade leading up to World War II marked the beginning of mass culture and a diverse popular literature that surpassed the old, familiar dime-store novels and detective stories.

In the introduction to the 1991 reissue of Ambler's first novel, *The Dark Frontier,* originally published in 1936, Ambler writes: "At the time my literary tastes were those of any other guilt-ridden young man who had rejected all orthodox religious texts in favour of the teachings of C. G. Jung, G. I. Gurdjieff, and Oswald Spengler. The novels of Dostoyevski and the plays of Ibsen were my bedside books." He goes on to say that the misery and madness of the time between the two world wars were "the stuff of dreams, even when the dreamer was as troubled as Strindberg or as haunted as Kafka."[1]

The triumph of Eric Ambler should be explored in terms of his infusing into the old secret-service adventure thrillers of John Buchan and Dornford Yates the ponderous freight of modernism. The terrors of the twentieth century were correctly seen by Ambler to be significantly different from the external forces of nineteenth-century naturalism—portrayed in Mary Wollstonecraft Shelley's *Frankenstein,* Charles Dickens's *Hard Times,* and Stephen Crane's "The Open Boat." Ambler astutely foresaw that Darwin, Freud, and Marx had monumentally shifted the focus of intellectual inquiry from extrinsic data to the intrinsic composition of the human animal. The angst of modern terror emanated from a fundamentally different view of the human being, one essentially opposite to the classical notions of rationalism and romanticism.

Gavin Lambert, author and screenwriter, identifies the crux of Ambler's contribution in his book *The Dangerous Edge*:

> Individuals are lost and isolated in a power struggle on a new scale. The physicist in *The Dark Frontier* not only forecasts the use of atomic weapons, but identifies the international cartel and the armaments firm as leading players in the war game. The big business corporation and the tycoon seem even more deadly than the totalitarian leaders with their blood purges and secret police. Financiers manipulate money and disturb whole economies. Industries produce immense stockpiles of guns and bombs. The profit motive creates the social chaos and the means of violence that lead to war. Although the Marxian argument reflects the intellectual left-wing climate of his time, Ambler uses it to convey a very un-Marxian feeling of personal helplessness.[2]

Eric Ambler's genius was to anticipate the horrors of the twentieth century in a literary and historical fusion in the novel of intrigue and espionage. Ambler was the first, in a long and ongoing line of literary craftspersons, to reveal the soul of the spy as the corrosive and vitiated soul of the twentieth century. Over the shoulders of the spy novelist loom the baleful figures of Franz Kafka, Feodor Dostoyevski, and Jung. Ambler's novels are the conduit of this tradition in both the spy genre and many nongeneric best-sellers of the past fifty years. In addition to his contributions to literary and cultural history, Ambler provides another valuable insight for readers and students of our time. From the vantage point of the mid-1990s, the contemporary world of danger and violence seems strangely centered once again on the familiar Amblerian territories of the Balkans and the Middle East. Eric Ambler and the living history of his fiction offer an ironic commentary on the claims of a "new world order" at the end of the post–Soviet and collectivist epoch. Having read Ambler, students in the 1990s learn that there is nothing new or orderly in the tragedy and disintegration of Yugoslavia or the Persian Gulf War of 1991.

A malaise of ignorance afflicts the current generation of young American students. This has been emphatically signaled by two surveys released in the early 1990s. The first, while attempting to measure geographical knowledge of American high-school students, found that few could locate the position of Florida on a national map. The second, more widely publicized, found that nearly one-third of all American high-school students believe the Holocaust might have been fabricated. Both surveys reveal a historical insularity among North American people and systems of education—an isolation deadly in a world defined by global economics and rife with ethnic hatreds. It is not too much to suggest that reading the fiction of Eric Ambler can provide perspective on such problems.

Moreover, the map of the mid-1990s is curiously reminiscent of the world map of the years leading up to World War I. The Ambler chronicles are a splendid tour of a world wrenched by the physical and metaphysical contortions of modernism. Those who read them may thus find themselves on a literary and historic pilgrimage to the echoing past that must be reshaped if the twenty-first century is to avoid repeating the mistakes of its predecessor.

While writing this critique, I have been painfully aware that it would be the third book published about Eric Ambler in as many years. Peter Lewis (1990) and Peter Wolfe (1992) have published astute assessments. I chose not to read them until my own manuscript was well into final stages, lest I corrupt the originality of my approach. This accounts for what some readers may find to be a paucity of references to Lewis and Wolfe. Consequently and furthermore, I have attempted to discuss Ambler's fiction without a dreadfully detailed accounting of plot; I have tried to give minimal sketches so as not to duplicate the Lewis and Wolfe work and at the same time devote more space to the lines of investigation and criticism that unfolded as I explored the theoretical and philosophical underpinnings of Ambler's fiction. To say that the approach that evolved is a Jungian study of Eric Ambler and the spy novel would be misleading; but I found, in time, as the Ambler's recurrent themes emerged, that Ambler needed to be re-evaluated in the light of the significant intellectual currents that shaped his own literary and psychological life. Friedrich Nietzsche, Jung, and Spengler were unmistakable influences.

Finding these linkages between Ambler's early and later fiction has been the major thrust of my work. As I state in the last third of the book, the persistent dwelling of critics on Ambler's earliest work as his finest has not been borne out by my investigation. The work from Ambler's middle and later years is connected to the prewar novels; I have attempted to illustrate how Ambler not only transformed the popular genre of the spy novel but also continued to change and transform the contours of popular literature well into the 1950s and 1960s. Like one of his marvelous metamorphic spy-protagonists, Eric Ambler developed as the author as trickster.

Acknowledgments

The collected papers of Eric Ambler in the Special Collections of the Mugar Library at Boston University were an indispensable source of reference and insight. I would like to thank Dr. Howard Gotlieb and his accommodating staff, especially Elizabeth A. Bolton and Katherine Kominis, for their cooperation and support during my visit in July 1992.

I would also like to thank Pat Browne, editor of the Bowling Green State University Popular Press, for permission to reprint parts of my essay on Eric Ambler from the 1976 *Dimensions of Detective Fiction.* Pat is also a friend and colleague whose fine work at the Popular Press has been an inspiration to those of us who are working in the fields of popular literature and contemporary culture.

I am deeply indebted to Joanne Foeller, of the State University of New York College at Fredonia's Creative Academic Support Services, for the magical wand she waves over software conversions and for her patience and ingenuity in producing and editing hard copy. The Interlibrary Loan Department of the College at Fredonia's Reed Library was also instrumental and persistent throughout the research process; I thank Margaret Pabst and Janet Ferry of that fine staff for many manual and electronic searches.

A sad but deeply grateful acknowledgment goes to the memory of my good friend, the late Will Rockett, dean of fine arts at the University of Wisconsin. Over lunch one day, one of many when Will was dean of arts and humanities at the College at Fredonia, he urged me to take a proposal for a book on Eric Ambler to G. K. Hall, then parent of Twayne Publishers. Will's untimely and unexpected death in September 1993 was a great loss to his many friends and colleagues. I had looked forward to showing him this book, the consequence of his collegial and scholarly advice.

Last but not least, I want to thank my family for their sustenance and patience. The constant inquiries by those who have left the nest—Rob, Anne, and Joe—about the progress of the book gave me continual impetus to show some results. To Jessica and Nicole, I gave daily thanks; each day, when getting off the school bus, they would come in and greet me with the peremptory salutation: "How many pages did you write today?" I was too fearful to present a negative response. And finally, in my wife, Debra, I acknowledge the compass that points to the bright directions in the dark crossings in the regions of mystery and love.

Chronology

1909 Eric Ambler born 28 June in London (Charlton).

1914 Family moves to Newstead Road, London.

1917 Ambler attends Colfe's Grammar School, London.

1924 Wins scholarship to the engineering program at Northampton Polytechnic, a branch of London University.

1925 Enlists in the Territorials, London Rifle Brigade.

1926 Hired by Edison Swan Electric Company, London, as engineering apprentice.

1927 Transferred to Lydbrook branch of Edison Swan.

1930 Hired as a copywriter for a London advertising agency (name unknown).

1936 *The Dark Frontier* published.

1937 Meets Alfred A. Knopf in London. *Uncommon Danger* published (reprinted in America as *Background to Danger*). Moves to France.

1938 *Epitaph for a Spy* and *Cause for Alarm* published.

1939 *The Mask of Dimitrios* published (reprinted in America as *A Coffin for Dimitrios*) and named book of the month in September by the *Daily Mail.* Ambler marries Louise Crombie in October.

1940–1946 *Journey into Fear* published in 1940 and named book of the month for July by the *Evening Standard.* Ambler serves in British Army, leads combat filming unit in Italy with American director John Huston, becomes assistant director of cinematography in the British War Office. Writes filmscript with Peter Ustinov for *The Way Ahead* (1944). Writes screenplay for the film *United States* (1945).

1947 Writes screenplay for *The October Man.*

1948 Writes screenplay with David Lean and Stanley Haynes for *The Passionate Friends* (distributed in America as *One Woman's Story*).

1950–1958 Writes screenplays for *Highly Dangerous* and *The Clouded Yellow* in 1950. In collaboration with Charles Rodda, publishes five novels under the pseudonym Eliot Reed: *Skytip* (1950), *Tender to Danger* (1951, reprinted in 1952 as *Tender to Moonlight*), *The Maras Affair* (1953), *Charter to Danger* (1954), *Passport to Panic* (1958).

1951 *Judgment on Deltchev* published. Writes screenplay for *The Magic Box.*

1952 Writes screenplays for *Campbell's Kingdom, Gigolo and Gigolette,* and *The Card* (distributed in America as *The Promoter*).

1953 *The Schirmer Inheritance* published. Writes screenplays for *Rough Shoot* (distributed in America as *Shoot First*) and *The Cruel Sea* (for which Ambler receives Oscar nomination).

1954 Writes screenplays for *Lease of Life, The Purple Plain,* and *Windom's Way.*

1955 Writes screenplays for *The Night-Runners of Bengal* and *Body Below.*

1956 *The Night-Comers* published (reprinted in America as *State of Siege*). Writes screenplay for *The Yangtse Incident* (also issued as *Battle Hell*).

1957 Moves to Hollywood at invitation of MGM. Writes screenplays for *A Night to Remember, The Guns of Navarone,* and *The Night-Comers.*

1958 Divorces Louise Crombie. Marries screenwriter Joan Harrison. Relocates with her to Bel Air. Writes screenplays for *Blind Date* and *The Eye of Truth.*

1959 *Passage of Arms* published. Writes screenplay for *The Wreck of the Mary Deare.*

1960 Creates CBS television series *Checkmate.*

1961 Brushfire destroys Bel Air home.

1962 *The Light of Day* published. Ambler is first writer (uncredited) to work on screenplay for *Mutiny on the Bounty.*

1963 *The Abilty to Kill and Other Pieces* published.

1964 *A Kind of Anger* and *To Catch a Spy: An Anthology of Favorite Spy Stories* published.

1967 *Dirty Story: A Further Account of the Life and Adventures of Arthur Abdel Simpson* published.

1968 Leaves California with Joan Ambler and relocates to Lake Geneva, Switzerland.

1969 *The Intercom Conspiracy* published.

1970 Writes screenplay for *Love Hate Love.*

1972 *The Levanter* published.

1974 *Doctor Frigo* published.

1975 Mystery Writers of America presents Ambler with its Grand Master Award.

1977 *Send No More Roses* published (reprinted in America as *The Siege of Villa Lipp*).

1981 Receives Order of the British Empire. *The Care of Time* published.

1985–1986 *Here Lies: An Autobiography* published in 1985. *The Army of the Shadows* published as limited edition in 1986. Relocates with Joan Ambler to London.

1991 *Waiting for Orders,* short-story collection, published.

Chapter One
"The Weird Multiplier": From Detective to Spy

When authors celebrate their birthdays, they often give appropriate gifts. When Kurt Vonnegut turned fifty, he wrote *Breakfast of Champions* as a present to himself. In 1989, at the time of his eightieth birthday and more than fifty years as a published writer, Eric Ambler wrote a new introduction to the first American paperback edition of his first novel, *The Dark Frontier,* originally published in 1936. The Mysterious Press edition, with a new introduction by the author, appeared in February 1991, and Ambler's following rushed to bookstores to learn more about the tight-lipped and elusive mystery writer. Once again, however, readers would discover that Ambler, like one of his fugitive and reluctant "wrong-man" heroes (innocent bystanders, caught through mistaken identity and drawn into the melee), had slipped through the noose. The curious historians of literary intrigue should have known better; after all, Ambler had managed to publish *Here Lies: An Autobiography* in 1985 while effectively covering the years of his life only up to 1953. Surely Ambler, by simply ignoring the later thirty years, was reminding mystery buffs of the famous Raymond Chandler quip that the ideal mystery is the narrative one would read if the end was missing.

The analogy of Ambler's career to the inapprehensible and variable nature of his dilettante-as-hero fits both the span and the composition of his literary output. As a writer Ambler has both the durability and metamorphic genius that sustain the agent provocateur in the field, along with an uncanny knack to foresee and link global events to his literature of international intrigue, politics, and espionage. Ambler's eighteen novels, published between 1936 and 1981, defy any monogeneric classification. His literary career was punctuated by long spells of military service and screenwriting; and yet there was a purposeful and seemingly predestinate incursion into the profession of writing thrillers.

In an interview with Joel Hopkins, published in the *Journal of Popular Culture* in 1975, Ambler revealed his then-conscious effort to transform the old right-wing, Brown-shirted garden variety of the secret-service adventure thriller. Asked by Hopkins about what led up to his now-famous flurry of literary activity between 1937 and 1940, which produced five novels (*Background to Danger, Epitaph for a Spy, Cause for Alarm, A Coffin for Dimitrios,* and *Journey into Fear*), Ambler responded: "What happened was simply having failed at playwriting, having failed as a songwriter, failed as an engineer, I looked around for something I could change and decided it was the thriller-spy story. I would do something different. The detective story genre had been worked over and worked over, but no one had looked at the thriller. It was still a dirty word. So I decided to intellectualize it, insofar as I was able. . . . I changed the genre and couldn't write the books fast enough."[1]

Before surveying the work of Ambler's predecessors, the "club and fuddy-duddy establishment" types whom Ambler "decided to turn . . . upside down" (Hopkins, 286), we would do well to investigate the circumstances that brought the young electrical engineering apprentice to the murky milieu of the literary thriller.

In 1935, Eric Ambler was in the advantageous position of being a trained engineer who could read the cryptic but alarming alphabet of the rapidly advancing science and technology of the modern era. The orthography of that alphabet signaled explicit and explosive changes in transportation, communication, and weapons delivery. A generation earlier Sigmund Freud had sensed the same impending doom when he saw his son Martin off to the front in World War I. Freud tried to console himself by saying that if the train took away, perhaps the telegraph would restore. But both Freud and Ambler, later in 1935, knew that the introduction of a new technology into the affairs of the world was about to produce radical and catastrophic change.

In his introduction to the reissue of *The Dark Frontier,* the novel in which he presciently—but not prescientifically—used the term *atomic bomb,* Ambler recalls his technoscientific literary debut as not terribly clairvoyant: "I lay no claim to special prescience. Having had a scientific education . . . I had read about the early work of Rutherford, Cockcroft and Chadwick in the field, and understood some of its implications" (*Dark Frontier,* xi). Ambler told Joel Hopkins: "[I]n 1935 the A-bomb was perfectly obvious. . . . Einstein had done the mathematics. There was bound to be an atomic bomb" (Hopkins, 289). Ambler's working knowledge of modern physics coupled with his artistic imagination led him to deduce that "the atomic bomb . . . was the work of a small team directed by one exceptional man of talent with a chip on his shoulder and grudges to bear" (*Dark Frontier,* xi–xii). Thus, in the instantaneous flash of the dawn of the nuclear age, Ambler astutely drew together the essential elements of the classic spy story: the nuclear Sword of Damocles that hangs over the global village; the delicate balance of terror introduced by a small, mobile weapon of vast destruction (this fragile equilibrium is later named the balance of power, or the cold war); and, finally, a later staple in the stories of Ian Fleming and all other "terrorist" dramas, the threat of the perverted genius of a spiritually deformed and monstrous villain.

At this beguilingly simple conjunction of scientific, aesthetic, and political elements there lies the genesis of the formula for the twentieth-century spy story. Ambler's self-deprecating and modest memoir of the moment is nearly as laconic as Jacob Bronowski's sketch of Isaac Newton's recalling the fallen Flower of Kent apple in his later years.[2] Ambler's matter-of-fact perspective belies the paramount importance of his literary trailblazing: "In 1935 I knew, theoretically, that E probably equaled mc^2, but I could not quite accept the numerically awesome consequences of the equation. I mean c^2 was such a huge and weird multiplier" (*Dark Frontier,* xii). The octogenarian writer proceeds to link the engineer's knowledge of physics to the remote memory of an eight-year-old boy in London:

> One evening in January 1917, when I was nearly eight and living in London not far from Greenwich, there had been an accident at a munitions plant two miles away across the river. They were processing TNT there; something went wrong and over fifty tons of the stuff blew up. Not even on the Western Front had there been such an explosion. It killed and wounded hundreds and flattened an entire factory area. The blast wave hit our street with great force and broke a lot of windows. I remembered the feel and sound of it. The idea of using a kiloton of TNT as a measure of explosive violence, even for a fictional nightmare bomb, seemed farfetched and possibly absurd. . . . [T]he welter of impulses, literary, political and commercial . . . drove me to start writing *The Dark Frontier* (*Dark Frontier,* xii–xiii).

In this "welter of impulses" lies the fortuitous confluence of personal experience and powerful global forces that combine in the trenchant insight of the young writer who seizes the moment to mold the formula of a genre (and several hybrids) of popular literature that survives to this day in the work of Ian Fleming, John Le Carré, Len Deighton, Robert Ludlum, and Tom Clancy, to name a few. Ambler found himself at the center of several forces that were about to impact a largely oblivious world; he himself could have easily retreated from this terrifying vision of that world's fragility. Like one of his "wrong-man" protagonists, he might have attempted an escape from violence, intrigue, and treachery, all fueled by the quantum leap of the "weird multiplier" of atomic physics. Instead, he consciously appropriated the shopworn vehicle of what he calls "the old secret service thriller as written by E. Phillips Oppenheim, John Buchan, Dornford Yates and their crude imitators; and I meant to do it by placing some of their antique fantasies in the context of a contemporary reality" (*Dark Frontier,* xiii).

The "weird multiplier" of Einsteinian mathematics—and the physical sciences—is but one aspect of the face of Ambler's "contemporary reality" in the 1930s, a decade that witnessed contortions and dislocations of the whole of intellectual modernism. The "weird multipliers" of the social sciences' constructions of reality were also known to Ambler through his close readings of Carl Jung, George Gissing, Friedrich Nietzsche, Oswald Spengler, and G. I. Gurdjieff, a Middle Eastern mystic residing in Paris. As always, in the infusion of literary realism and naturalism, Charles Darwin and Sigmund Freud are only a short step away—never too far from the clinical laboratory of modern social science.

Once again, in his introduction to *The Dark Frontier,* Ambler keenly recounts his insistence on historical accuracy and his attempt to "intellectualize" the older, anemic spy story. Ambler attests to the historical accuracy of a seemingly simple detail in the novel that alleges the presence of a gunsmith's shop in Paris's Latin Quarter in the 1930s. Ambler confesses that many years later, when rereading *The Dark Frontier,* he had laughed aloud at the very notion of a gunsmith in the old Boulevard Saint Michel. Then he recalls his numerous conversations with French traveling salesmen (Ambler traveled frequently to France in the early 1930s, before moving there to write from 1937 to 1939); each admitted that he carried a small pistol while plying his trade. Furthermore, each confessed to Ambler that their fathers, the "old-fashioned men" of a certain age, liked to carry a gun when they were out driving their automobiles.

Ambler intuitively and deftly discovered the "weird multiplier" of modern technology: in the trappings of the adventure thriller, he fused social custom, technology, primitivism (the atavistic violence), and the Jungian apparatus of condensation and transfer.[3] The combination of automobile and handgun had touched some raw nerve of territorial atavism and the need to conquer and control—both technological devices had amplified and extended the old agencies of human power. Ambler recognized the depths of that residual and enduring agency and its infinite increase in power in the atomic weapon. Ambler's singular contribution to the spy story—and, arguably, to popular literature—lies in seeing that the lofty world of academic theory (why are so many of Ambler's long line of wrong-men heroes professors by vocation?), abstract equations, and intellectual history has profound links to the "secret self" of the individual psyche. For Ambler, the weight of modernism is borne heavily by the individual who is agonizingly aware of the burden of knowledge. That knowledge is power, to be sure; but is the power of the spy a reprise of the Faustian temptation, which may well lead to ultimate self-knowledge—and self-destruction?

A brief biographical background of this versatile engineer turned mystery writer reveals an even greater range of knowledge and skills useful to adventure narrative. In many surprising little ways, Eric Ambler was poised for the role of recording and interpreting the assemblage of incongruous events that threatened the "old world order" of 1935.

The London of Ambler's birth in 1909 was somnolently basking in the last rays of the setting sun of Victorian hegemony and order. Not far from where he was born, a gargantuan ocean liner was being built that symbolized the far-flung power of British rule. Nearly fifty years later in 1958, Eric Ambler would write the screenplay about the *Titanic*'s maiden voyage for the movie *A Night to Remember.* Ambler himself was by then renowned for being the writer who had predicted a brave new world of fearsome technological might and dark treachery—a world that prospered in violence and the spread of new empires, all without the presence of the formerly ubiquitous Union Jack. The world, and its merchants of power and destruction, had long moved on to *Sputnik,* ICBMs, and the cold war. Though Eric Ambler and the *Titanic* had come into the world at nearly the same time and place, Ambler not only survived the famous luxury liner but came to chronicle the demise of the era it symbolized.

The son of Alfred (Alf) Percy Ambler and Amy Madelin Andrews, Eric was born on 28 June into a family of music hall and vaudeville entertainers. His father had been reared in Salford, Lancashire, but the family finally settled in Lee, in southeast London. When they met at a "Finsbury smoker," Alf Ambler "took a fancy to Amy Andrews, the pretty nineteen-year-old soprano,"[4] whose father was a cabinetmaker in Totenham. Married in 1906, Ambler's stagestruck parents performed in troupes for "concert parties," billing themselves as "Reg and Amy Ambrose."

As a teenager, Eric was keen to join his parents' troupe, called "The Whatnots," but they wished for him a more respectable and substantial career than show business. Ambler told Joel Hopkins: "My father insisted that I not go on the stage or have anything to do with the arts, which he had, so I thought, naturally, I should go the other way. I think a lot of people decide too early what they want to do. I did. I won a scholarship to London University, but from the moment I became an engineering student, I was a potential dropout because I began to try and write plays—not novels—and lyrics to songs" (Hopkins, 286).

Thus, instead of the music hall, the venue for young Eric's early education was the nearby secondary school, Colfe's Grammar School, which he entered in 1917. In his autobiography, he states: "Colfe's saw its primary task as that of educating us to matriculation standard and seeing that we passed that examination as well as our abilities allowed. After that—well, yes, there was a sixth form (*Here Lies,* 43). But it was likely not the sixth form that enabled the young Ambler to witness firsthand the materials and character studies for later literary realism. Elleston Trevor has argued persuasively that Ambler perhaps acquired his real education in a form that was in such old schools as the one Ambler attended designated as *The Remove.* It was, Trevor says, between the third and lower fourth forms—a segregated level for boys who could not be controlled. "The Remove was less of a melting-pot than a garbage can, and its denizens can later be found securely in the police records across Europe and the Middle East. A few less imaginative souls became prime ministers, perhaps as a gesture of atonement."[5] Ambler himself says, "I was a juvenile delinquent. I used to steal cars and such, but I was very good in science" (Hopkins, 286).

Eric Ambler was so good in science, in fact, that at age fifteen he scored a perfect 100 percent in chemistry and physics for the university examination at the University of London, and he was awarded one of only four of the prestigious scholarships. He chose to study engineering, but even from the beginning there was evidence of irrepressible literary talent:

> When I arrived at Islington on the day of the exam there was hardly room to move. For the four scholarships there were nearly two hundred applicants, mostly sixth-formers from London area grammar schools. One or two had small moustaches. It was very depressing.

> It was weeks before the results of the exam came through and during them I had lost some of my interest in engineering. . . .
>
> When a letter arrived saying that I had won the top scholarship, I was pleased, naturally, but not perhaps as pleased as I should have been. I was already searching in secondhand bookshops for Everyman editions of the plays of Ibsen. Fired by . . . a London performance of Pirandello's *Six Characters in Search of an Author,* I had decided to become a playwright. (*Here Lies,* 63)

For most people engineering studies and the continental naturalist-realist theater would have been divergent tracks; but for Ambler these twin passions would converge.

The engineering student found the curriculum easy and, like most students in that situation, found the burden of guilt as a truant easier yet to deal with in time. Ambler initially spent his study time at the library of the Institute of Electrical Engineers; but, as he himself later revealed, "The Institute was on the Thames Embankment only a few minutes walk from the Law Courts. Soon I was spending whole mornings in the public galleries of the King's Bench Division or the Criminal Division of the Court of Appeal." He soon found himself forsaking the scientific journals for the "foxed thirty-year-old copy of Winwood Reade's *Martyrdom of Man.* This was the book that Sherlock Holmes had casually recommended to Watson during their early days in Baker Street, and it was because of that recommendation that I had first been drawn to it" (*Here Lies,* 65).

During this whole period of engineering studies, distracted but richly inspired by his excursions to the Law Courts and his reading in the theoretical underpinnings of the British tale of detection, Ambler was stagestruck, and theater remained the central beacon of his vocation (or avocation) to the arts. He attended plays incessantly and took to writing down certain scenes that seemed to work particularly well. He applied (unsuccessfully) for work as a stage electrician; he haunted the tea shops and pubs frequented by stagehands. Diversion piled on diversion; at the suggestion of a friend, Ambler enlisted in the London Rifle Brigade regiment of the Territorials (akin to the American Army National Guard) in late 1925. This connection to the British military establishment would turn out to be important in 1940 at the outbreak of World War II; Ambler would eventually find himself in the inner circle of the military escort for Winston Churchill (where he once unabashedly corrected the prime minister's knowledge of a film cast) and, subsequently, in the company of American film director John Huston.

In 1926, the inevitable finally happened. Eric Ambler left his engineering studies to take advantage of an apprentice engineer job with the Ponders End (London) works of the Edison Swan Electric Company. In *Here Lies,* Ambler explains that the depression was looming, and many engineering graduates were out of work. Transferred in 1927 to Lydbrook, in the scenic valley of the River Wye, Ambler supervised for a time the manufacture of colliery cable—the cable-works itself was near the Waterloo, the deepest pit (mine) in England. In that summer at Lydbrook, Ambler wrote the first two chapters of a never-to-be-completed novel about his father. His writing eventually came into play at Edison Swan when he was appointed to the publicity department staff. After this turning point, Ambler would never again ply his engineering trade, except as the technically astute writer of spy stories.

From 1929 to 1930, Ambler launched a brief career in the footsteps of his recently deceased father as a music hall comedian, writing his own materials. He continued to pursue his habit of intense reading: "[T]he librarian of the Public Library at Addiscombe . . . would let me have six books at a time. . . . It was on his shelves that I found Jung's *Psychology of the Unconscious* and *Collected Papers.* Jung led me to Nietzsche and *The Birth of Tragedy.* In the same part of the library I found my way to Spengler" (*Here Lies,* 92). Such tomes were strange primers for a music hall performer.

In the early 1930s, Ambler worked in the copy department of a London advertising agency. The atmosphere bristled with literary ambition. At the same time, Dorothy L. Sayers was working at a rival London agency, Benson's, and turning out high-quality detective stories. Many of the copywriters in the burgeoning business of public relations had also been to Oxford and Cambridge and were exponents of collectivist and socialist ideologies. Ambler himself notes in *Here Lies:* "The techniques of commercial persuasion may be seen from the outside as differing only slightly from those of political subversion" (98).

Ambler's politics of this period (1930–36) have received a good deal of attention. In his 1972 history of the thriller, *Mortal Consequences,* Julian Symons writes: "In the six novels he wrote before the outbreak of World War II, [Ambler] infused warmth and political color into the spy story by using it to express a Left Wing point of view."[6] Likewise, in his 1978 *Sleuths, Inc.,* Hugh Eames describes the socioeconomic milieu of Britain in the early 1930s: "London seethed with new social solutions, and Eric

Ambler was engaged."[7] Eames portrays Ambler as a capitalist by day in the ad agency and a radical revolutionary by night. He quotes Ambler from years afterward: "I was ready for the barricades. Anything anti-Fascist, I was on its side. I was a very far left wing socialist. I thought this was the light and if only I could get clued-up on dialectical materialism I could go far" (Eames, 151). In their 1987 study, *The Spy Story,* John Cawelti and Bruce Rosenberg find a sustained message of anticapitalist politics in Ambler's work, from the 1930s all the way to *The Levanter,* published in 1972: "*The Levanter*'s theme—of the destructive power of aggressive capitalists—is a restatement of the political philosophy expressed in *Background to Danger* [1937]. Despite his disenchantment with Russia and her satellites, he remains something of a 'leftie.'"[8]

During the period from 1930 to 1935, Ambler engaged in literary activity—a prodigious amount, in fact. Asked in a 1981 interview with Jean W. Ross if he was "writing while . . . doing the other things," Ambler responded, "Oh yes. I wrote lyrics and anything that I could get performed. I had a couple of plays put on."[9] In fact, although all unpublished, Ambler had produced before his twentieth birthday two novels, four plays, and several songs. By his middle twenties, he had made a total of £25 from his writing; in 1936, with the publication of *The Dark Frontier,* he would double that overnight.

With a steady income as a copywriter, Ambler was able to afford some travel. His journeys would feed into later writing. Gavin Lambert has chronicled Ambler's meanderings throughout the Mediterranean, the fabled sea that beckoned the maturing writer from well back into his early education in the classics as a youth on Sandhurst Road: "He gravitated towards the Balkans and the Middle East, following the Orient Express route to Belgrade, Athens, Istanbul. He reconnoitered Beirut and Cairo, and in Tangier he met a blowsy motherly Central European refugee who ran a beach cafe and turned out to be a spy" (Lambert, 106).

In *Here Lies,* Ambler tells a tale from his travels, both distressing and stunning, that underscores his attraction to intrigue, treachery, and danger and his power of imagination. Having taken a fortnight's holiday from the ad agency, Ambler spent ten days traveling on a slow freighter to and from Marseilles. The four days spent ashore proved to be testimony to his survival skills as well as to his uncanny connection to a sense of place. While staying at a bed and breakfast on the Canebiere, he gets relentlessly stiffed at a game of pokerdice by a bartender. Hungry and broke, much like his later "wrong-man figures," the young Ambler distracts himself by planning an assassination:

> I was in a corner room overlooking the intersection of the Canebiere and the side street where the bar was. Outside my window there was a narrow balcony with a wrought-iron grille. Through the spaces in the grille I could see the roadway at the point where the barman would cross to the tram stop. With an imaginary rifle in my hands I lined up a space in the grille with a brass curlicue on the base of the standard lamp. I waited and watched, with the intersecting curves of the tramlines in my sights, for nearly an hour. The barman never came and I returned to James Joyce. It was quite a shock, a few weeks later, to see on the newsreels that same piece of the Canebiere with the intersecting tramlines. The spot I had chosen for my sniper shot at the barman had also been chosen by the Croatian assassin of King Alexander of Yugoslavia. (*Here Lies,* 114–15)

The Croatian assassin managed to kill both the king and the French foreign minister, before himself being killed by a bodyguard. Ambler's reaction was: "If he had taken my room . . . and used a rifle he might have had a chance of getting away." The whole incident served to reinforce Ambler's sense of connection to a genre of popular literature that he was about to consciously seize and turn upside down: "I saw the newsreel several times and cut out news pictures of the scene. I felt oddly guilty, but also pleased. In the Mediterranean sunshine there were strange and violent men with whom I could identify, and with whom, in a way, I was now in touch" (*Here Lies,* 115).

When Eric Ambler set out to write a novel in 1935, he focused his sights on a specific form of fiction: "The only kind of popular novel about which I had strong feelings was the post-war thriller. . . . [I]t had nowhere to go but up" (*Here Lies,* 120–21). He had intended the novel to be "a parody of a thriller. That was what I had meant it to be when I had started out. It changed as I went along; and, no doubt, as I began to learn how such stories could be well told" (*Here Lies,* 122). The advance on *The Dark Frontier* was £30 from Hodder and Stoughton; Ambler's career as adventure-thriller-spy novelist was launched with its publication in 1936.

It is Ambler's life from this point on that has sparked the most interest, yet it oddly shrinks in proportion and known detail compared with his first twenty-five years. Perhaps it is one more "weird multiplier" in the life of the author; like one of his "displaced person" (amnesiac and/or multiple-persona) protagonists, the real Eric Ambler (according to the opinions of his traditional critics) is the flash-in-the-pan, best-selling novelist who moved to Paris in 1937, wrote six blockbuster thriller novels that transformed the genre of espionage and detective fiction, and then disappeared into the British Army in 1940.

The real Ambler fades, according to popular criticism, as the next thirty years are telescoped into the standard allusions to his having emerged from the war as a screenwriter who in dilatory fashion wrote a few inferior novels and short stories, with a hiatus from writing novel-length fiction between 1940 and 1951. Additionally, the usual accounts record two marriages; one divorce; an Oscar nomination for the screenplay for *The Cruel Sea* in 1953; a move to California and work in Hollywood from the late 1950s to the late 1960s; a catastrophic house fire in Bel Air in 1961; and, finally, the return of the "real Eric Ambler," with *The Light of Day* in 1962, and with a high-water period from 1969 to 1974, launched by *The Intercom Conspiracy* of 1969.

In actuality, throughout the intervening years between the benchmark dates of literary production, Ambler was a prolific writer of filmscripts. Between 1946 (the year of his discharge from the British Army) and 1958 (the year of his move to California), Ambler worked for a British film company, J. Arthur Rank's Cine-guild. His nineteen screenplays include not only *The Cruel Sea* and *A Night to Remember* (1957) but the *The Guns of Navarone* (1957) and *The Wreck of the Mary Deare* (1959).

In addition to the film work, between 1952 and 1957 Ambler covered notorious cases in the courts and current events (including the infamous Kim Philby disappearance) for the British print media. He traveled widely, and slowly but certainly gravitated back to the old domain of the adventure-spy-international-intrigue thriller. On his return to novel writing, Ambler comments: "I had not written a book for ten years and in the Army had lost the habit of a concentrated and solitary writing routine. The process of its recovery was slow. Besides, during those ten years the internal world which had so readily produced the early books had been extensively modified and had to be re-explored" (*Here Lies,* 226). Despite this modest disclaimer, at about this time Ambler not only wrote and published three novels (*Judgment on Deltchev,* 1951; *The Schirmer Inheritance,* 1953; and *State of Siege,* 1956) that reintroduced him to the postwar readers of popular fiction but also, under the pseudonym of Eliot Reed, collaborated with the Australian writer Charles Rodda on the publication of five books in England and America.

For Ambler, the return to novel-length fiction was a heart-warming homecoming: "For me [*Judgment on Deltchev*] represented a happy return to writing thrillers" (*Here Lies,* 229). If the novels of the 1930s had been inextricably linked to their period, the era of the Popular Front and the Left Book Club, the 1951 *Judgment on Deltchev* was received by critics as well as old and new readers as an "anti-Stalinist socialist novel" (*Here Lies,* 229). Ambler was caught in a hail of abusive letters from his former following for becoming "a traitor in the class war struggle" and "a Titoist lackey." In reality, Ambler had matured as both person and artist; politically, he seems never to have forgotten the shock and the disillusionment of discovering in 1939, when in Paris, the news of the signing of the Molotov–von Ribbentrop nonaggression pact between the Soviet Union and Nazi Germany.[10]

This articulation in the novels of the 1950s of a point of view different from that of the younger writer is essential to understanding the growth of the artist as spy-novelist. His middle to late novels contributed to the genre's gradual buildup to Le Carré, Deighton, and Anthony Burgess: their aggregate world of the fully developed spy novel is a place of absolute treachery where ideology is the refuge of only knaves and fools.

In the late 1950s, as Ambler was moving away from film work, he found himself moving to America and a brief period of enchantment with television. He stayed in America for approximately a decade, living in Bel Air (until a brushfire destroyed his and Joan Harrison Ambler's home and belongings in 1961) and Los Angeles. The call back to novel writing is the point at which Ambler closes his autobiography, *Here Lies.* He ends with an excerpt of a speech given to the British Film Academy, in which he describes himself as one of the lucky few writers able to "fertilize the sacred cow." In thinly veiled terms, he describes his return to fiction writing: "It will not be long before he is back working in a medium in which he can be fully creative; in which he can forget for a while the sacred cow and its attendant male nurses, and function again not only as a father to the child, but as mother, doctor and midwife also" (233–34).

While the "sacred cow" of film and television popularized Ian Fleming's work and the pyrotechnic approach to the literature of espionage in the 1960s, Eric Ambler went quietly back home and nursed back to robust health the anemic orphan of the genre abandoned in year gone by. In 1961, after traveling again in Turkey, Greece, and the Middle East, Ambler began writing *The Light of Day.* The first three chapters were destroyed in the Bel Air fire, but Ambler rewrote them and the novel was published in 1962 and then successfully filmed in 1964 as *Topkapi.*[11] Throughout the 1960s, Ambler continued to write novel-length fiction and edited two anthologies of favorite detective and spy stories. His introduction to the 1964 anthology *To Catch a Spy* is a first-rate analysis of his and others' work in that then rapidly developing genre of popular literature.

Around 1972, Eric Ambler was "re-discovered" by both the expanded popular reading audience and the hotly pursuing critics of a genre that had been "Bonded" by Ian Fleming's formula to mass culture consumption because of a cold war in Europe and a hot little war in southeast Asia. All told, Ambler may safely be viewed as having written through three distinct phases. The first period was the celebrated pre–World War II flurry of sensationally popular and famous six novels. The second began with *Judgment on Deltchev* in 1951, followed by *The Schirmer Inheritance* in 1953 and *State of Siege* in 1956. Critics have found the hallmarks of this postwar "second period" to be the diminution of Ambler's customary adventure and violence and the intellectually attractive addition of refined character development, social and political verisimilitude, and a maturation of moral subtlety. Gone are the one-dimensional ideologues from the collectivist 1930s; in their place are ambivalent characters with morally murky perspectives that are more closely akin to the Quixotic purists of Le Carré and Graham Greene or the black humorist vision of Anthony Burgess in *Tremor of Intent.* The third period of Eric Ambler is the "re-discovery" from 1972 to about 1977, highlighted by the return of Charles Latimer (from the high-water *Dimitrios*) in *The Intercom Conspiracy.*

In this study I do not provide a conventional portrait of Eric Ambler as "received" by his critics, nor do I offer a strictly chronological review of the Ambler canon and its temporal unfolding of thematic issues and increasingly complex narrative devices. Rather, my analysis reveals an Eric Ambler who pursued cohesive themes and points of view throughout nearly fifty years of fiction and essay writing. Rather than dwell on the stages of Ambler's development as a writer and thinker, I focus on the motifs and materials that draw the Ambler canon into a fairly well-patterned and neatly structured series of discourses on subjects that held his intellectual and literary attention from the late 1920s until his last publication in 1992. In addition, to develop these lines of inquiry fully, I do not examine his last three novels. This decision does not reflect the quality of those novels, but—given the coverage in Peter Lewis's *Eric Ambler* (1990) and Peter Wolfe's *Alarms and Epitaphs: The Art of Eric Ambler* (1993)—it has given me the freedom to illuminate the remarkably patterned themes and structures of the majority of Ambler's works.

Chapter Two

A Spy in the House of Ratiocination

What was the state of the genre when Eric Ambler decided to do for the literature of espionage what Dorothy L. Sayers had done for the detective novel? Was the state of the art confined merely to the Bolshevik-baiting, crypto-Fascist snobs with Brown-shirt outfits in the clubhouse lockers? What are the early twentieth-century origins of a literary genre that has, through the agency of Eric Ambler and a very few others, seized the imagination of both popular and self-proclaimed elitist reading (and film) audiences for the last seventy years?

The literature of espionage and political intrigue is rooted as far back as tales in the Old Testament. The first spy story in written literature is contained in the Bible, in the Book of Numbers. Moses had led the Israelites out of bondage in Egypt and halted the exodus in the wilderness. Jehovah himself instructed Moses to send spies into Canaan. Moses personally selected his secret agents—one from each tribe—and he chose only the most capable men for the expedition. The spies returned and reported that Canaan was a land flowing with milk and honey.

The secret agent and spy genre, however, did not establish itself until well into the twentieth century. Just as the detective was able to galvanize the perspectives of the late nineteenth-century social sciences and calculate the design of a clockwork universe,[1] the spy has emerged as the modern representative of an outdated and sometime unheroic individualism that is capable of challenging a menacing world of conflicting organizations, ideologies, and technologies.

The pedigreed line of spy stories has its true genesis in 1903, with the publication of Erskine Childers's *The Riddle of the Sands.* At almost the same time, Joseph Conrad was writing novels of international intrigue and espionage—especially *The Secret Agent* in 1907. Conrad's early and perceptive treatment of espionage, along with his deeply psychological probings of the human psyche, has persisted in various strains through today.

Before the genesis of modern espionage literature is awarded to the twentieth century alone, a brief but relevant history of two established nineteenth-century authors, who made significant forays into the spy genre, should be surveyed. James Fenimore Cooper published *The Spy* in 1821; and Henry James brought out a tale of international assassination in 1886 with *The Princess Casamassima.*

The publication of his second novel, *The Spy,* brought James Fenimore Cooper the recognition he had initially sought with *Precaution. The Spy* has the American Revolution for its setting, and the ambiguities that pervade the novel accurately prefigure the same central conflict as that between Judge Temple and Leatherstocking in *The Pioneers,* his third novel.[2] The forest and open land in *The Pioneers* suggest a complex moral issue of contrived ownership versus free use; *The Spy* poses similar oppositions. The British family, the Whartons, must choose between American principles of freedom and their vested wealth in British property. The elder Wharton opts for property, and later nearly loses all. Harvey Birch, the double agent, is "the example of positive value in the book" (Ringe, 31). He expects no personal gain from the war and, because of his concealed identity, wins not even recognition and prestige.

The disparity between appearance and reality is an ingredient of the modern spy tale that Cooper mastered early in this nineteenth-century tale. Wherever the reader turns, the appearance of things is deceptive and further layers of reality are unearthed. The Whartons conceal a corrupt reality beneath the appearance of virtue while the spy must conceal his virtue beneath an apparent corruption and is reviled and distrusted by all. Behold all of the thematic elements of a Le Carré novel—in 1821. Cooper's concept of amoral passivity will reappear many generations (of both readers and changes in the genre) later, in Anthony Burgess's *Tremor of Intent* (1966).

The other nineteenth-century prototype of the spy novel, *The Princess Casamassima,* was faulted by James himself as being partly responsible for his declining popularity in the late 1880s. In 1888, James wrote to his friend William Dean Howells that he feared his reputation had suffered because of his last two novels—*The Bostonians* and *The Princess Casamassima.*[3] The perspective of time and distance may now indicate that James's assertion was correct, but only because *The Princess Casamassima* was too advanced for its day.

The Princess Casamassima is a novel of international intrigue, political assassination, and foreign espionage. The central character, Hyacinth Robinson, is the agent provocateur, the subject of the usual Jamesian probing of psychological motives. The submotifs of a theory of art and the workings of guilt in the human psyche, integral elements of the modern tale of espionage, appear here. *The Princess Casamassima* may well be awaiting a literary resurrection when considered as the most significant precursor of the modern spy novel. James's technique and thematic subtleties were paralleled quite closely by the efforts of Joseph Conrad in the following generation, and a direct line of descendence seems to flow from James, to Conrad, to Maugham and Ambler, and finally to Le Carré.

James employed the theme of universal betrayal in *The Princess Casamassima*—a theme of contemporary import—but his central conflict is, more significantly, the mutual exclusion of two vocations; he focuses on the schism between a contemplative life devoted to art and a pragmatic life dedicated to civic action. Hyacinth Robinson is torn between the two. He possesses all of the sensitivity of the artist, with that special weltanschaung of a life committed to art, yet he is enlisted to commit the crime of political assassination. It is a suicidal mission, and Robinson in full awareness pledges himself to death. Lionel Trilling most aptly characterizes this forerunner of the modern spy: "Hyacinth's death, then, is not his way of escaping from irresolution. It is truly a sacrifice, an act of heroism. He is a hero of civilization because he dares to do more than civilization does: embodying two ideals at once, he takes upon himself, in full consciousness, the guilt of each. He acknowledges both his parents. By his death he instructs us in the nature of civilized life and by his consciousness he transcends it" (Trilling, 90).

The two ideals are the beauty of art and the beauty of a political science in good government. But the respective guilts are there, also. The impracticality (or simple absence of action) of the life of art cannot be reckoned with; and the setting right of social and political ills must somehow always lead to revolution, violence, and possible anarchy. It is the classic dilemma faced by Prometheus, Antigone, Hamlet, and Faust. It is also the dilemma of the cold war spy who retains a certain reservoir of humanity and who seeks to "come in from the cold." But there is no entrance, just as for Sartre there was "no exit." The dilemma demands a moral choice, and neither alternative offers a respite, or an entrance back into normal life.

Trilling's description of Hyacinth Robinson is a remarkable character study of Eric Ambler's later string of "wrong-man" protagonists who inadvertently step over the threshold to a moral action—and, even once having returned, find that their view of the world is never again so simple or far removed from some action of import. Le Carré would later invent the professional spy who became disillusioned with all ideology—and its concomitant ethical discovery of the need to act. For James and Ambler, however, the very notion of action had an existential significance. In fact, Eric Ambler, after having written six novels and on his way to action on the eve of World War II, wrote to his wife in December 1940: "Once in a book, I quoted Nietzsche—'action has no sense, it merely binds us to existence.' I'm sure I never realized how acute an observation that is."[4]

The next effort at writing a modern spy novel (that is, after 1900) was made by an established British writer fifty years of age and in his thirteenth year as a published author. In 1907, Joseph Conrad knew well that his reading of the political pulse of Europe was accurate when he produced *The Secret Agent.* In an essay on the evolution of the modern spy story, Ambler states that "*The Secret Agent* is one of Conrad's acknowledged masterpieces, and it is difficult to discuss other spy stories of that period in the same breath."[5] Conrad also published *Nostromo* in 1904 and completed *Under Western Eyes* by 1911; both novels address a broad range of political intrigue and anarchism. *The Secret Agent* also contains a study of these latter socially relevant topics, but the protagonist, M. Verloc, also happens to be a British subject who is an agent provocateur in the employ of the Russian Embassy. This trilogy of Conrad's closely parallels the fiction of Henry James and the Dostoyevskian tradition in Russian fiction.

In writing his now famous introduction to *Under Western Eyes* in 1951, Morton Dauwen Zabel not only produced a classic essay on Conrad but also emerged as one of the first literary critics of the spy genre. Zabel comments on Conrad's linkage with James and Dostoyevsky and says: "*The Secret Agent* of 1907 is now readily recognizable as a pioneer in its genre—the tale of political intrigue, espionage, and moral anarchism in modern Europe which has become a typical mode of fiction in our age of *Machtpolitik,* scientific violence, and 'international evil.'"[6]

The Secret Agent tells of a plot by a group of London anarchists to blow up the Greenwich Observatory. The plan is hatched in a foreign embassy (presumably Russian). Adolph Verloc, a shopkeeper and consort with anarchists, is charged with the mission of executing the demolition by inciting the socialist aspirations and proletarian dreams of his revolutionary protégés. Conrad derived this drama of London espionage in large part from an actual attempt to explode the Greenwich Observatory in 1894. "That novel of intrigue, anarchism, and treachery in the London of the 1890s, with its plot of terrorists, bomb-makers, and agents provocateurs manipulated by an unnamed foreign power in the interests of inciting the western European nations" was Conrad's full portrayal of the two evils he feared most—radical socialism and anarchism (Zabel, xxiv–xxv). In Conrad's tale, the mission fails and Verloc is murdered by his wife, before she drowns herself. As in all spy stories, betrayal emerges from all sides and little remains but the certainty of life's unpredictability.

Conrad's enduring creation in *The Secret Agent* is the character of Professor X—a truly postmodernist nonideologue who espouses a kind of nihilism. In the whole novel, Professor X is the sole character who is incapable of betrayal, precisely because he comes to reject all ideologies and systems, all slogans and political clichés. In chapter 4, Professor X enunciates his "neutrality": "You revolutionists . . . are the slaves of the social convention, which is afraid of you; slaves of it as much as the very police that stands up in the defence of that convention. Clearly you are, since you want to revolutionize it. It governs your thought, of course, and your action, too, and thus neither your thought nor your action can ever be conclusive. . . . You are not a bit better than the forces arrayed against you."[7]

But Professor X does not prefigure the Ambler and Le Carré characters trying to "come in from the cold" war of conflicting ideologies. The professor lacks the warmth of humanity to thaw the frozen chill of intellectual remove, and instead places his hope for the future in dynamite. "Give me that for a lever, and I'll move the world," he says (Conrad, 251).

R. W. Stallman interprets this thematic nihilism as a subtle affirmation of life itself: "Theories—scientific, political, sociological, economic, psychological—all are reduced to zero by Conrad's diabolic irony. What protection against life that we devise consists of superstitions, myths, theories, conventional conceptions of reality, systems of creeds, codes of behavior by which society is manipulated and controlled; in sum, all that the muddling intellect contrives. The nihilism of *The Secret Agent* ends in a covert affirmation of the supremacy of life. Could we but manipulate reality so that what happens happens as predicted—but no! Time-Now is the Unpredictable, life in all its irrational particulars; including X the unknown event."[8]

The manipulators are the human agents who twist people and events through cant and betrayal. In *The Secret Agent,* however, Conrad depicts "sudden holes in space and time" (80), and ideologies and the political abuse of language cannot stand up to the human conscience and to guilt—life itself. In the final analysis, *The Secret Agent* is not a genuine spy novel. Like Henry James, Conrad explored the psychological approaches to the modern novel wherein the protagonists are characters who also happen to be spies. In many ways, both James and Conrad anticipated Ambler's and Le Carré's internalized etchings of guilt, betrayal, and treachery in the soul of the Everyman-spy; but the spy novel would have to endure fifty years of plot gyrations, pyrotechnics, and chauvinistic tirades before the emergence of the mature genre in the midtwentieth century.

In 1915, John Buchan published *The Thirty-Nine Steps,* the classic espionage story of World War I. Buchan continued his serial treatment of the adventures of Richard Hannay with thirty-odd novels and short stories; as the depression deepened, however, Hannay's right-wing political leanings fell out of favor with many readers, and the plots never developed beyond the dime-store fare of gratuitous chance and circumstance. Buchan and Hannay have, nevertheless, seen many reprintings of *The Thirty-Nine Steps* (1915), *Greenmantle* (1916), and *Mr. Standfast* (1919). All three novels (along with the agent-protagonist) were considerably more successful than the sortie by Arthur Conan Doyle and Sherlock Holmes into World War I international intrigue. The great detective was too old and tired for the strenuous games of espionage, and he mercifully retired to his bees and opiate dreams.

Graham Greene, in a memorial essay, best sums up John Buchan's contribution: "More than a quarter of a century has passed since Richard Hannay found the dead man in his flat and started that long flight and pursuit—across the Yorkshire and the Scottish moors, down Mayfair streets, along the passages of . . . building . . . rooms and country houses, towards the cold Essex jetty with the thirty-nine steps, that were to be a pattern for adventure-writers ever since. John Buchan was the first to realize the enormous dramatic value of adventure in familiar surroundings happening to unadventurous men."[9] Greene illustrates the point by quoting Hannay: "Now I saw how thin is the protection of civilization. An accident and a bogus ambulance, a false charge and a bogus arrest—there were a dozen ways of spiriting one out of this gay and bustling world" (Greene, 104).

Because of Buchan's influence, the spy story perpetuates both the horror of civilization's fragility and the delicate equilibrium of society's security.

The spy genre reached another important milestone in 1927, when W. Somerset Maugham decided to fictionalize, in print, his memories of his World War I service as an agent of the British Intelligence Department. In *Ashenden, or: The British Agent,* Maugham unwittingly shaped the main formulaic pattern of the genuine tale of espionage and thus directed the course the genre was to take for the next sixty-five years. Maugham's profound influence lies precisely in the formula he created in *Ashenden,* which was followed closely by Eric Ambler and Graham Greene through the 1940s. Since then, Ian Fleming, John Le Carré, Len Deighton, Robert Ludlum, and Tom Clancy have employed certain elements of Maugham's formula. Even Anthony Burgess's "postmodern" spy novel, *Tremor of Intent,* has given "eschatological" (Burgess's term) perpetuity to the original *Ashenden* pattern.

In its simplest form, the Maugham-*Ashenden* formula has evolved as follows:

1. A master spy, usually a retired military man, recruits an innocent, nonprofessional spy for a "job" and introduces him to the dirty business of spying.
2. The unsuspecting recruit is a writer or a professor—an observer of human nature—who is reluctant; but he overrides his misgivings and accepts the mission.
3. The dilettante does well, succeeds through his cleverness and wit; but all the while he remains an aloof observer who despises the bloody, bumbling work of espionage.
4. The mission is jeopardized often; capture either occurs or is several times imminent; but the neophyte spy ultimately accomplishes the mission and acquires new knowledge and wisdom of the ways of the world.
5. Upon return, the newly baptized-by-fire agent rejects any possible continuation in the service and resolves to return to normal life. His lesson is always something of this nature: the real world—and life itself—is much more complicated than the easy and untested affirmations of the armchair ideologue. Nevertheless, the novice opts to return to a quiet study.

Apparently without having read *Ashenden,* Ambler employed many of these elements in his first novel, *The Dark Frontier,* written in 1935. In his autobiography, Ambler tells of a luncheon with Eileen Bigland, a writer and editor, soon after the publication of the novel. When she asked Ambler what models he had used for *The Dark Frontier,* he responded with a litany of names that "wandered through Gogol and Compton Mackenzie to Pirandello and James Joyce" (*Here Lies,* 123). She nodded glumly in return and stated tersely: "Try Somerset Maugham." Ambler, who was already well into his next novel, *Background to Danger,* took her advice and found a kindred spirit and parallel path in *Ashenden.* Ironically, Maugham cited in his preface to *Ashenden* the example of Guy de Maupassant, and Ambler thereby found a hidden but corroborative source for his probing of the "contemporary reality" in this subtle infusion of the Zola-directed school of continental realism and naturalism. Ambler's reading at this time included the novels of Dostoyevski and the plays of Ibsen; fit company for the Maugham dramatis personae.

Eric Ambler's significant accomplishment in the spy genre revolves around his transitional hybrid form. His literary predecessors belong more properly to the mode of detective fiction than to the burgeoning tales of espionage as prefigured in Buchan and Maugham. To be sure, the exotic geography of Buchan and the variegated characterizations of Maugham are to be found in the early Ambler novels. But Ambler's peculiar type of novel is still a crossbred spy/detective permutation of the detective story that happens to have a spy as the central character and/or foreign intelligence agents as the antagonists. The quintessence of the Ambler spy/detective tale is the novice's inadvertent involvement in a plot of international intrigue and his subsequent loss of innocence as he follows the "accidental" clues provided. The method of detection is logical and deductive; thus, Ambler's typical novel might employ parts of Maugham's formula. The methodological frame of the Ambler novels, however, bears the imprint of the older tale of ratiocination.

As a device for realism, the amateur as protagonist succeeds for Ambler by reducing all of the angst of international intrigue to a very personal level. A reader's distance is maintained when a dangerous situation is ably managed by the professional spy. But Ambler gets the edge on suspense by making his spy/detective an average person, and the reader identifies easily. In this sense, the Ambler novel has always been more of a "thriller" than the later professional-spy novels of the cold war era typified by Fleming and Le Carré. It is easy to imagine oneself in the predicament of an Ambler hero.

A philosophy of history is always as important in an Ambler novel as the social context in which the novel is written: one complements the other. Ambler may have retained some of the shell of the old detective genre, but the nut of the new material is the freight of intellectual history that weighs on both the immediate and the global implications of the villainy involved. As noted earlier, the menace of a science and technology that threaten world order is what brought Ambler to the thriller. In an assessment of the two cultures of science and human values, Ambler anticipated the writings of C. P. Snow and Jacob Bronowski, who were also driven by the nuclear revolution into a brooding numbness that needed to evaluate the health of the two cultures. Ambler's intellectual questions have always been: What happens to human values when science and technology change the equation of control, and perhaps even alter the very notion of civilization? What happens to the definition and development of "culture"? Informed by Nietzsche and Jung, Ambler's definition was from the beginning a clearly Darwinian view of the human species as "an ape in velvet."[10]

A poignant example comes from *A Coffin for Dimitrios,* written in 1939, on the eve of World War II. This was also Ambler's "breakthrough" novel, which insured his reputation as a critically acclaimed writer of thrillers. The novel reveals a condensation and articulation of Ambler's penchant for a philosophy of history that reflects his readings of Jung and Spengler: the point of view insists that Europe (and Western civilization) had reached a stage of such decadence that it was bent on self-destruction. One of the minor ironies of the novel consists in the fact that Latimer, the spy/detective protagonist, is both a writer of detective fiction and a lecturer in political economy in a second-tier British university. When he moves beyond his secure sphere as academic observer into the role of participant in actual melodrama and real intrigue, he learns a lesson in politics and economics. Or, more precisely, he learns about the inadequacy of theory and the deadly realities of unclear choices in an atmosphere of murky morality and economic pragmatism. Like the rest of the world on the eve of World War II, Latimer finds himself dragged unceremoniously into the grim realities of the twentieth century:

> In his room, Latimer sat down by the window and gazed out across the black river to the lights which it reflected and the faint glow in the sky beyond the Louvre. His mind was haunted by the past. . . . Three human

> beings had died horribly and countless others had lived horribly that Dimitrios might take his ease. If there were such a thing as Evil, then this man. . . .
>
> But it was useless to try to explain him in terms of Good and Evil. They were no more than baroque abstractions. Good Business and Bad Business were the elements of the new theology. Dimitrios was not evil. He was logical and consistent; as logical and consistent in the European jungle as the poison gas called Lewisite and the shattered bodies of children killed in the bombardment of an open town. The logic of [Michelangelo's] *David,* Beethoven's quartets and Einstein's physics had been replaced by that of the *Stock Exchange Yearbook* and Hitler's *Mein Kampf.*[11]

In the outside world of experience, Latimer had become an eyewitness to the brutality and selfishness that produce poison gas, assassination, and aerial bombardment—all faithfully executed under the sacrosanct aegis of nationalism and capitalism. The immoral and reprehensible actions of the greedy individual become blurred and somehow justifiable amidst the unquestioned activities of bureaucratic government and big business; where law-abiding individuals fear to tread, corporate entities can ride roughshod. Politics and economics—the new theologies—reign supreme, and Dimitrios, the international outlaw, is in his own logical way the incarnate paradigm of the age. Very much like the American Upton Sinclair, some thirty years earlier in his best-selling novel *The Jungle,* Eric Ambler appropriated the Darwinian metaphor for the naturalist's portrayal of economic struggle. For Ambler, however, the house of carnage was not the meat-packing industry of Chicago but the gas-blistered battlefields of World War I and the coming slaughterhouse of World War II. In his own microcosmic psychopathic behavior, the now-dead Dimitrios had merely emulated the mightier social and economic contortions of the larger agents of history.

Latimer therefore returns to the inner world of art—in particular, to detective fiction. The detective story is but an extension of Michelangelo's *David* and Beethoven's quartets, a work emanating from the last audible message of the old harmony of the spheres. The detective story grows out of a world of limited systems, made up of deductively ordered facts and theorems. It is an enclosed cosmos congenial to the refugee from an environment of armed hostility and imminent chaos.

All of this signifies the raison d'être of the literature of espionage. The major premise of Ambler's argument resides in the dangerously thin veneer of protection that civilization offers to the modern world. The ages of Medieval faith and Renaissance decorum are past: Charles Darwin, Freud, Sir James George Frazer, and Spengler have triumphed. The world of the detective—the interlocking, visible puzzle pieces of Isaac Newton, Auguste Dupin, and Sherlock Holmes—is inadequate when faced by the snarl of technological warfare. Therefore, the day of the spy had dawned. The detective writer and the ballistics engineer had to temporarily assume characteristics of the bestial Dimitrios and other villains in order to survive. There is a little of Dimitrios to be found in everyone—violence, betrayal, and treachery are the legacy in the global village. The spy/detective is the hero metamorphosed from the Victorian secret sharer who must reconstruct the shattered world of rationalism. Even though Latimer was able to retire to his academic chamber and return to the Victorian parable of certain detection of all transgression, Eric Ambler and the events of 1939 did not permit popular fiction to repose placidly in a calm of "phony war."

In his introduction to the 1991 *Waiting for Orders,* his only collection of short stories, Ambler discusses the darkening events in Europe in late 1939 and the influence of these events on his life. After marrying Louise Crombie in early October in Croyden, he found himself in essentially the same position as every other young man at the time—waiting for the call to military service, or "waiting for orders." In the twilight hours of the first half of the twentieth century, Ambler "wrote six cosy little murder mysteries," all based on his empirical research in forensic medicine. Ambler describes his planning of the short stories: "A suitable master detective was needed. He would have to fit into small narrative spaces. His entrances and exits must have a clear pattern. He must belong noticeably to the times we were living in. He must be a refugee" (*Waiting,* 5).

In this short series, Eric Ambler bids farewell both to his first period as a writer and to a world that will never again be so simple, in his worldview, as to be contained in "small, narrative spaces." The real refugee was the metamorphic protagonist who had necessarily discarded the definite shape of the detective for the formlessness of the secret agent. Eric Ambler had been all along a spy in the house of ratiocination.

Chapter Three

Dark Crossings: Twilights of the Gods and the Psyche

The modern spy novel had its genesis in the study of the psychic apparatus of the twentieth century. From the very title of his first novel, *The Dark Frontier* (1936), Ambler owes much of his formula for the spy novel to the work of Carl Gustav Jung, a writer and thinker who attracted Ambler's attention from his youthful days of truancy in the engineering program at the university. Ambler himself provides the essential clue in the epilogue to the first novel, where he discusses the incidence of dual personality and amnesia as described in Jung's early work. Ambler opens the epilogue by stating, "Such cases of dual personality do occur. C. G. Jung in his *Collected Papers on Analytical Psychology* describes the case of a young German girl who was subject to periods of amnesia, or loss of memory, during which she exhibited a completely different personality" (*Dark Frontier,* 273).

An examination of that 1917 volume of Jung papers reveals an extraordinary series of psychological investigations into the "pathology of so-called occult phenomena." Jung defines the areas of "rare states of consciousness" as the interstitial regions of psychopathic deficiency that include the conditions related to "narcolepsy, lethargy, *automatisme ambulatoire,* periodic amnesia, double consciousness, somnambulism, pathological dreamy states, pathological lying, etc." Jung proceeds to depict these conditions as being nearly indistinguishable from the major "regions" of the so-called "neuroses." Jung then makes the curious comment: "Recently the view has even been maintained that there is no clean-cut *frontier* between epilepsy and hysteria" (italics added).[1]

Ambler, it would seem, appropriated this idea of the dark regions of the mind for his amnesiac/dual personality hero of *The Dark Frontier,* Professor Henry Barstow. In the opening pages of part 1, titled "The Man Who Changed His Mind," Ambler renders the musings of Barstow, as a prelude to events on the morning of his amnesia attack, in the very language of the Jungian idealized self, conflicted by strange and dark fantasies:

> His day-dreaming had always been of statesmanship behind the scenes with himself as the presiding genius, of secret treaties and *rapprochements,* of curtain intrigue conducted to the strains of Mozart, Gluck and Strauss, with Talleyrand and Metternich hovering in the background. Queer, too, how dreams of that sort stayed with you. One half of your brain became an inspired reasoning machine, while the other wandered over dark frontiers into strange countries where adventure, romance and sudden death lay in wait for the traveller. (*Dark Frontier,* 8–9)

The dark frontiers of John Le Carré and Len Deighton are the dangerous back alleys of love and betrayal in East Berlin (and central London); before them, in the wake of the early clinicians, Eric Ambler trudged through a similar landscape rutted by the deep recesses of the modern psyche.

The years immediately preceding Ambler's first try at a literary thriller witnessed the publication of a flurry of books and pamphlets in London on the subject of amnesia, dual personality, and parapsychology. The impetus for this sudden and widespread public interest in these subjects in Western Europe was the intellectual climate following World War I. Not only did the war result in the many cases of shell shock and battle fatigue that intrigued the burgeoning school of clinicians (in the line of succession of Jean Martin Charcot, Freud, and Jung), but it brought into the West a population that brought with it Middle Eastern and Eastern European religious and philosophical teachings. One example, acknowledged as an influence by Eric Ambler, was the Armenian-born mystic George Ivanovitch Gurdjieff. In 1925 Parisian habitués of the Grand Hotel de la Paix attended on the pontifical Gurdjieff, who for years afterward engaged the attention of an international group of aficionados of Eastern mysticism.[2] In London, shrill condemnation of Gurdjieff was issued by 1920s literati D. H. Lawrence and Wyndham Lewis; but such a response on the part of the London intelligentsia hardly affected the popularity of books on the topics in the early 1930s.

In relation to Ambler's use of amnesia and dual personality themes in *The Dark Frontier* are two books that appeared in London in 1932 and 1933. Published anonymously in 1932, a well-traveled memoir of an amnesiac titled *I Lost My Memory: The Case as the Patient Saw It* provided the novel point of view of the patient himself—an apparent victim of shell shock as an officer of a line regiment in World War I. The memoir was authenticated by a preface written by the attending physician. In 1933 came *Persons One and Three,* the case study of another world war "somnambulistic" veteran, authored by Shepherd Ivory Franz, a psychology professor at UCLA. The book jacket claimed that the investigation "casts a fascinating light into one of the dark chambers of human psychology."[3] The use of the "dark chamber" image recalled the case studies by Jung in 1917 and anticipated the title of Ambler's novel.

If Ambler owes a debt to either of these works, the former would be the better bet. Besides the obvious borrowing of the patient's point of view, other interesting parallels exist between *I Lost My Memory* and *The Dark Frontier.* The surname Carruthers appears at a key point in the memoir; in *The Dark Frontier,* when Barstow suffers amnesia as the result of an automobile accident, he emerges from the wreck as supersleuth and spy, Conway Carruthers. Also, one of Carruthers's trademarks is his perpetual puffing on a pipe; the alleged real-life narrator in the memoir is possessed of very few recollections of his other personality, but a love of pipes and tobacco connects his dual personages. The anonymous narrator goes to some lengths to explain the "tobacco memory" and puzzles over the explanation:

> My taste for tobacco had come back with a vengeance, and . . . I have retained a glorious memory of the contentment of the hour.
>
> I . . . suppose that the long use of tobacco had produced an actual need for it in my metabolism. Such a need would not depend on memory for its continuance, and it might very well remain unrecognized until time and the hour brought the possibilities of a noble fulfillment.[4]

At the conclusion of *The Dark Frontier,* Ambler employs sustained smoking of a familiar pipe and tobacco in the moving scene where Barstow is identified (surreptitiously by the American journalist) as the same personage as one Conway Carruthers, the British operative who saved the world from nuclear proliferation and extortion at the hands of a Balkan state. In a chilling scene of recognition, the journalist, William Casey, is given the vantage of a double point of view, prefiguring what is to become a classic ironic device for Eric Ambler:

> The man on the bed lay on his back, his fingers lightly clasping the sheets across his chest. I looked at his head turned slightly to one side, at the grey-streaked hair disordered by the pressure of the pillow. Then I looked at the long fingers I had so often seen forcing tobacco into a battered pipe with nervous dexterity and my mind went back to a moment in which those same fingers, grasping a heavy German automatic, were being raised towards the head that now lay peacefully on a clean, white pillow. (*Dark Frontier,* 270–71)

Here is an indication of the fine line between social order and primal savagery; the hand that packs the pipe of repose is easily capable, in altered states of consciousness and other circumstances, of becoming the hand that toggles the nuclear trigger. Jung had spoken of "idealized" states of alter-ego transfer, and Ambler surely found in the new depth psychology emerging between the wars—a new popular culture—enough of the shadows that suggested many less-than-ideal alternative personality traits and types.

The figure of the amnesiac picaro provides a device that may serve as a neat set of bookends for the fifty-year span of Ambler's work between 1936 and 1985. His 1985 autobiography, *Here Lies,* opens with the in medias res episode of Ambler's supposed automobile accident in Switzerland, from which he allegedly suffered a period of amnesia. The accident and amnesia in the autobiography parallel the events precipitating the metamorphosis of Professor Barstow into Agent Carruthers. It is not clear whether Ambler is telling the truth or playfully suggesting the interpenetration of art and life—mirrored in the title *Here Lies.* He goes so far as to conclude the narration of the event by having a Swiss neurologist declare: "If you wrote in a novel about such an accident and stated that so little damage was done, nobody who knew anything would believe you" (*Here Lies,* 19).

Thus, with the suspension of general disbelief, Ambler not only begins his "life story" (as opposed to the suggestion of the obituary narrative also in the autobiography title) but also mimics the incredible events that inaugurated his literary career. Drawing on an ancient tale (Rip Van Winkle), bolstered by modern evidence from experimental depth psychology, Ambler created a modern global hero: the secret agent, the man of many identities, guises, and even states of consciousness.

The Dark Frontier

Julian Symons's assessment in *Mortal Consequences* that Eric Ambler's first novel "is the least important of his books" exemplifies the traditional disregard in which critics hold *The Dark Frontier* (Symons, 238). According to Symons, and a generation of critics, the only noteworthy feature of Ambler's first thriller is the prophetic anticipation of the first atomic bomb. Admittedly, Ambler had yet to perfect his formula, but he did deliver to a popular audience the connective elements of Jungian psychology and Nietzschean philosophy in the form of the amnesiac hero and the spiritually deformed villain.

The Dark Frontier begins with a prefatory "Statement of Professor H. J. Barstow, F.R.S., Physicist, of Imperial College, University of London" (1). This statement is rendered in the language of a legal deposition, but the point of view is markedly reminiscent of *I Lost My Memory*. Like the anonymous narrator of the memoir, Professor Barstow reveals the indisputable evidence, collected by the police and medical authorities, that indicates a period of time in his life of which he has no recollection. For Barstow, five weeks in late spring of the previous year are a blank. Also like the amnesiac patient of the memoir, Barstow writes movingly of the strange sensation of reading about himself as a distant character in an unknown text.[5] In Barstow's case, the narrative is further enhanced by foreign travel and international intrigue.

Professor Barstow succinctly describes his station in life before his disappearance: "Forty years of age and a bachelor, I am, by profession, a physicist and, during the four months preceding April 17th, my services had been retained by a British government defence research department to make a feasibility study of a set of proposals for a new weapon system employing an ultra-high explosive" (2). The intense strain of these four months of work sends Barstow to the medical adviser. A long holiday is prescribed.

Setting out alone in his automobile for a fortnight in Cornwall, Barstow stops at midday in Launceston for luncheon at the Royal Crown Hotel. The seemingly chance encounter at lunch with an arms merchant, Simon Groom, from Cator and Bliss (an international arms manufacturer) is the impetus for the professor's forays into the dark frontiers of wartime big business and his own repressed consciousness. For all of his brilliance as a scientist, Barstow is unaware of the complex depths of both frontiers he is about to enter. A kind of holdover from the eighteenth century, personifying its vision of the orderliness of nature, he is about to be thrust into a twentieth-century nightmare of total loss of control over the natural world, with its latent disorder and destructiveness.

Ambler deftly constructs the juxtaposition: "Professor Barstow did everything methodically, whether it was applying the laws of electrodynamics to a case of electronic aberration or combing his Blue Persian cat. His very appearance spelt order. His lectures before the Royal Society were noted and respected for their dispassionate reviews of fact and their cautious admissions of theory. . . . The truth of the matter is, perhaps, that he distrusted his imagination because it told him things he did not wish to believe" (7–8). By the end of the novel, Ambler has shown Barstow's transformation into a man who no longer trusts any orderly accounting of events and who has only theories and speculation to use in the quest for his identity and the meaning of actions.

Barstow's journey from innocence to disillusion provides evidence for a claim Ambler has made about the nature of his first novel since the time of its publication: that it is a parody. Critics have assumed that Ambler aimed the parody at the old Edwardian secret-service pulp fare; he did, but he achieved more. In his introduction to the reissue of *The Dark Frontier* in 1991, Ambler furnishes a more relevant explanation of his target—Britain's prime minister Stanley Baldwin and his smug Edwardian innocence. Ambler says: "In 1928 Prime Minister Stanley Baldwin, the trusty, pipe-smoking [another amnesiac in Ambler's private joke?], true blue Tory statesman who had seen England safely through [several crises] . . . threw caution to the winds. He praised a novelist publicly" (xv). The novelist was Mary Webb, author of *Precious Bane* and other regional Shropshire landscape novels. Ambler aptly summarizes the rage that fueled his own parodic impulse: "Why, then, did I find *Precious Bane* so insufferable? Mainly, I think, because of its pretentious breast-beating. All that blending of human passion with the fields and skies that Mr. Baldwin so admired was for me no more than an untimely and artless revival of the Victorian poets' pathetic fallacy. . . . The incidence of psychoneuroses and violent crime among Shropshire yokels may have been exceptional at the time, but the attempt to render it as high tragedy was a mistake" (xvi).

Thus, Ambler decries the absurd naivete of saccharine Edwardian sensibilities; while the rest of Europe was being palpably transformed by psychoneuroses and violence on the massive scale of capitalism, fascism, communism, and ethnic hatreds in the Balkans, the prime minister concerned himself with a novel whose themes Ambler perceived as parochial and melodramatic.

In *The Dark Frontier,* while Baldwin and Britain sleep, Barstow awakes to the experiential call to action from the collective unconscious. His awakening reflects the unmistakable influence of Jung. By Ambler's own accounting, he freely used the Jungian apparatus of depth psychology for his primer in constructing modern characters with multilayered psyches. Barstow's transformation is heralded in Jung's essay, "The Assimilation of the Unconscious," part of the *Collected Papers on Analytical Psychology* referred to in the epilogue to *The Dark Frontier.* Barstow's megalomaniac awakening to the idea that he is to "save civilization" is described by Jung:

> Outer attractions, such as offices, titles, and other social regalia are not the only things that cause inflation. These are simply impersonal quantities that lie outside in society, in the collective consciousness. But just as there is a society outside the individual, so there is a collective psyche outside the personal psyche, namely the collective unconscious, concealing . . . elements that are no whit less attractive. And just as a man may suddenly step into the world on his professional dignity ("Messieurs, a present je suis Roy"), so may another disappear out of it equally suddenly when it is his lot to behold one of those mighty images that put a new face upon the world. These are the magical *representations collectives* which underlie the slogan, the catchword, and, on a higher level, the language of the poet and mystic.[6]

Jung elaborates on this state of "psychic inflation" as an extension of the personality beyond individual limits. Jung employs the terms "godlike" and "superhuman" and proceeds to define this inflated state of consciousness as related to Arthur Schopenhauer's "world as will and idea" (seeing the world as one's "picture book") (Jung 1956, 153). Eric Ambler thus found his way via Jung to Schopenhauer and Nietzsche, as he combined the elements of amnesia and the dark frontier of the collective unconscious in the transformation of the professor into the inflated, but beneficent will to power in the agent Carruthers. But what would happen, as Jung suggests in the same text, if the will to power should prove pathological? Ambler provides that other side in the person of the scientist Professor Kassen. In this spiritually deformed figure, Ambler delivers the hellish half of the collective unconscious—the demonic will to power that might incur the dissolution of both inner and outer worlds (see Jung 1956, 156–58).

Simon Groom, the unsavory arms merchant from Cator and Bliss, is the purveyor of the Nietzschean philosophical connection to the clinical perspective of the superhuman nature of "psychic inflation." Groom is the satin-smooth voice of seduction; he approaches Barstow with the rationalist and positivist justification for war:

> War, with its demands on mankind for offensive and defensive instruments, rocks the cradle of most constructive endeavors today. The warships of yesterday produced the liners of today. The ferro-concrete fortifications of the battle area produced that wonderful new building they are putting up in North London. Bearing those facts in mind,

> Professor, what, I ask you, is the logical field for the development of a new and incalculable force such as that of applied atomic energy? (14)

Groom goes on to taunt Barstow with his intimate and secret knowledge of the production of an atomic bomb in the small Balkan country of Ixania (an imaginary place but, as shown below, probably Bulgaria). The internationally known Ixanian physicist Kassen is revealed by Groom to be the genius behind the bomb. But the genius is deformed by a flaw in character; having been rejected by the prestigious laboratories of the world, Kassen nurses a grudge against the world. Groom informs Barstow that three weeks earlier, a small Kassen bomb, the size of a Mills grenade, moved more than a thousand tons of rock. Simon Groom then becomes the first in a long line of Ambler villains to quote Nietzsche:

> "Ixania," he said, "is a state with national aspirations. You may question the right of so insignificant a strip of unproductive country to attempt to give rein to such ambitions. It depends upon your philosophy. A disciple of Rousseau would say 'yes' with all the fervour of his sentimental creed. For myself, I incline more towards the Nietzschean view. . . . Now, as if in answer to her prayers, she [Ixania] has produced a man of genius. Her peasants are wretched, her bourgeoisie is corrupt and her government is ineffectual; yet by a freak of biology or destiny, or both, this thing has happened." (16)

As the first exponent of Nietzschean principles in the Ambler canon, Groom articulates the consummate value of power in a new world order (or disorder) and the universal basis of that value in the collective unconscious. The force of modernism is contained in Groom's last line; whether it is biology or psychology (the referent was "destiny"), the lessons of Darwin, Freud, and Jung are corroborating the valorization of power, and the will to power, as enunciated by Nietzsche in the latter half of the nineteenth century. The common denominator in these sciences and social sciences is the relationship to nature; note how Groom belittles the romanticist Rousseau. The conquest of nature is the key to the will to power in the future; whether Kassen is the sport of evolution or a product of the psyche, he is the superman who represents all of the modern knowledge about nature and human nature. And as Nietzsche pointed out in *The Birth of Tragedy,* art must now give way to science and will.

In that 1872 essay, Nietzsche attempted to interpret Greek art and drama in light of Schopenhauer's philosophy. The myth of Dionysus (the wine maker, the reveler) becomes for Nietzsche the representation of his principle of the eternal return. Nietzsche avers that Dionysus torn to pieces is the promise of new life; nature and energy will be forever born anew as these irreducible elements of life rise afresh from destruction. Dionysus signified for Nietzsche the ever-shifting finite energy of the universe, perpetually regenerating itself in an endless cycle of life and death, order and chaos. Nietzsche identified the source of this energy as the will to power. Dionysus is juxtaposed with Christ, for Christianity, according to Nietzsche, is opposed to this superabundant energy. Later on, in 1881, nine years after *The Birth of Tragedy,* Nietzsche came to conceive of the "eternal recurrence" as a separate metaphysical principle.[7] This distinction in Nietzsche's progressive formulation of power was not lost on Eric Ambler, who returns to Nietzsche in his third novel, *Epitaph for a Spy.* In fact, Ambler's philosophical villain in that novel condemns Nietzsche for a loss of courage. (Ambler's use of Nietzsche will be covered more fully in the later discussions of *Epitaph for a Spy* and *Journey into Fear.*)

In *The Dark Frontier,* Simon Groom, the first of the Ambler apocalyptic soothsayers, appears as the mythical Prometheus of many guises—the modern agent of chaos and destruction, all in the name of progress and positivism. Groom delivers the modernist message that the disarray of the old order must be reshuffled according to new laws and principles (the Promethean fire of the atom is suggested by Groom). Barstow the physicist unwittingly becomes the prime witness to the unlevering (or exploding) of the mechanical world order of Newton by the atomic power of Einsteinian and Nietzschean relativism. In addition, Barstow accompanies Jung to the outposts of psychology and consciousness; the sum effect of this experience is a harrowing glimpse into disorder and the dark periphery of the twentieth century.

Verisimilitude is a prerequisite for the effectiveness of parody. And the case of Ixania, the fictitious country that attempts to develop an atomic bomb, is also a thinly veiled parody of the powder keg that was the Balkan states in the 1930s. In all likelihood, Bulgaria served as the model for Ixania. The turbulent events in Bulgaria between the world wars include an Agrarian party, internal reforms, the assassination of a key party leader, a royal dictatorship, and a turn toward fascism. From 1934 to 1935, shortly before Ambler began writing the novel, Bulgaria saw a military coup by two colonels working in concert with the monarch, Boris III. In 1930, Boris had married Giovanna, the daughter of King Victor Immanuel III of Italy. From 1935 on, the real ruler of the country was Boris, who modeled his government on Italian fascism. Boris and the colonels put severe restraints on constitutional government and abolished the political parties. Earlier, in 1923, the leader of the Agrarian party had been assassinated. Many of these elements are mirrored in the factional strife in Ixania, most of them thinly disguised. Even Giovanna appears as the mysterious Countess Magda Schverzinski and at the end of *The Dark Frontier,* the refugee royalty finds shelter in Italy.

If the verisimilitude, along with its concomitant parody, of Ambler's first novel was lost on the first generation of critics, the book found an eager audience and one very important ally in America. The year was 1936, and as Ambler was rewriting the last chapters of his second novel, *Background to Danger,* his agent at Curtis Brown informed him that Alfred A. Knopf, the famous American publisher, was in London and wanted to meet Ambler. Knopf had read *The Dark Frontier* and was interested in publishing Ambler's forthcoming novels in the United States. Ambler maintained a friendly relationship with Knopf through the years and was secured an international audience from the time of their meeting.

What was it that Alfred Knopf picked up on in the fledgling novelist's first effort? Even Ambler's accounts of Knopf's sponsorship have a ring of incredibility. A key to Knopf's early and lucid appraisal of Ambler perhaps lies in his handling of the next Ambler novel. In *Here Lies,* Ambler relates the minor flap at Hodders, his British publisher, over the title of *Background to Danger:* "For some reason that I never understood Hodders objected to the word 'background' in the title. So, in all English-speaking countries except the United States, the book was published as *Uncommon Danger*" (127). Ambler suggests Hodders was trying to avoid direct reference to a backdrop of imminent trouble: "The year was 1936, the year in which Italy invaded Abyssinia, Civil War broke out in Spain and Hitler ordered the German Army to reoccupy the Rhineland" (124). Alfred Knopf was unafraid of the correlations.

The final ingredient in *The Dark Frontier* that signals Ambler's innovation and perhaps drew Knopf's attention was the inclusion of an American journalist as the narrator for the second half of the book. Ambler admits that the sudden shift to the newsman as narrator "was simple desperation on my part. It was this intrusive late-comer who made it possible for me to resolve all the story problems I had created for myself earlier on by breaking, or ignoring, other sound storytelling rules" (*Here Lies,* 121–22). Most of the narrative problems to which Ambler is referring concern the construction of a single hero who happens to be amnesiac; another observer had to be added. Ambler's choice of an American journalist represents one more instance of his prescience. Since World War II the journalist has become acknowledged as an eyewitness to history. Moreover, the rising dominance of the print and film media (coincidentally, Ambler was to meet John Huston six years later, while both produced military documentaries during the war) has presented audiences in the past fifty years with a wholly different form of eyewitness accounting—the cinematic and the photographic. Ambler had accidentally, perhaps as he had with the atomic bomb and modern depth psychology, arrived at a fortuitous moment in the juncture of technology, modernism, and narrative development. His experimentation was the path of the future. It would seem that Alfred Knopf was a fellow traveler at the same intersection.

Background to Danger

Reviewing the Ambler autobiography for the *Partisan Review* in 1987, David Lehman noted that one of the hallmarks of Ambler's fiction, "a cool, understated prose style that efficiently serves the exposition of his plausibly complicated plots," can be dated from his second novel, *Background to Danger* (1937).[8] As Ambler himself recalls: "Reviewers in many places said that I had written a new, more realistic and better kind of thriller" (*Here Lies,* 127).

In *The Spy Story,* Cawelti and Rosenberg see *Background to Danger* as having an elaborate set of parallel devices and events in common with John Buchan's *Thirty-Nine Steps* (102–10). While one might agree substantially with their assertion that Ambler's second novel "owes much to Buchan's *Thirty-Nine Steps*" (102), one must ultimately recognize and accept their concession that "None of this accumulation of similarities proves that Ambler based" his novel on the Buchan work (105). In fact, Ambler developed in his second novel a pattern that has roots in his first, namely, the use of a journalist (who becomes the protagonist this time) and the uncanny knack of forecasting geopolitical events (this time relating to oil, long before Middle Eastern cartels and Arab embargoes). Cawelti and Rosenberg are on target when they cite Ambler's additional continuation of an original theme: the condemnation of war as big business and the product of international greed and capitalism. Ambler's education in socialism, by his own avowal, had consisted of the party speaker in Hyde Park on Sundays and his reading of George Gissing and *New Grub Street* (*Here Lies,* 125).

Background to Danger begins not in the back streets of some Balkan labyrinth but in the central business district of London, where a very important meeting of the Pan-Eurasian Petroleum Company's board of directors is convening. Ambler is still very much the astute student of engineering and science, as he invades the corporate boardroom with the dirty business of espionage and bribery. The background to this danger is the engineer's knowledge of the supply and technological disposition of material resources. The novel is prefaced by a brief but essential excerpt from a report by the World Petroleum Institute. As an engineering apprentice in Britain's mining industry, Ambler had learned of the crucial relationship between natural resources and national security.

The business at hand in the boardroom of Pan-Eurasian Petroleum (which owns 35 percent of Cator and Bliss, the munitions firm carried over by Ambler from *Dark Frontier*) is that company's efforts (mostly through bribery) to obtain Rumanian oil concessions have been unrewarded. The chairman of Pan-Eurasian informs his board that now a scurrilous pamphlet has been published by the United Socialist Party of Rumania, titled "The Vultures Gather." "Reds!" yells one of the directors, a Lord Welterfield. And when the chairman proposes the introduction of a man whose services will help bring about the oil concessions, the board approves. Minutes later, in another room, the services of a Colonel Robinson, whose real name is Stefan Sarizda, as a "propagandist" are retained by the chairman.

Sarizda's strategy is simple but ingenious. If he can get hold of the Soviet contingency plans for the invasion of Rumania, he will merely supply these plans to the Rumanian press (once again, Ambler intuits the burgeoning power of the print media). Despite the fact that these are outdated contingency plans, and Russia has no real intention of invading Rumania in 1937, this disclosure will undoubtedly catapult Rumania into turmoil. Big business will count on the ejection of the socialists and the hegemony of the right-wing, bribable elements who will seize control in Rumania and allow the leases to go out to Pan-Eurasian.

About agents provocateurs like Sarizda and the international capitalist concerns he represents, Ambler permits this Marxian sermon, later in the novel, from the mouth of the benevolent Soviet Colonel Andreas Zaleshoff:

> They say that persons like Al Capone and John Dillinger are products of America's corrupt administration and clumsy law-making. Sarizda and his kind must be the products of the world business system. . . . You see, your business man desires the end, but dislikes the means. He is a kind-hearted man. He likes an easy conscience. He likes to think that the people he exploits are pleased and happy to be exploited. He likes to sit in his office and deal honestly with other business men. That is why Sarizda is necessary. For at some point or other in the amazingly complicated business structure of the world, there is always dirty work to be done.[9]

Eric Ambler was the first writer of the thriller to decry capitalism, or any other ostensible ideology, in his progressive movement toward the articulation of the spy's enterprise as "dirty work." As Ambler implies, this dirty work is the coin of big business, and the two sides of that currency are appearance and reality.

Into this web of intrigue steps the penniless journalist, Kenton. Having been impoverished by a game of pokerdice (based on Ambler's own experience at Marseilles), Kenton is on his way to Vienna from Nuremberg to borrow some money from a friend. Aboard a local train outside Linz, he is unwittingly drawn into the higher-stakes game of espionage dirty work. Like his predecessor, Barstow, Kenton quickly discovers big business's duplicity, and he soon undergoes the Ambler transformation of a protagonist from hunted to hunter. The kindly Zaleshoff is on hand to rescue him from the grips of Sarizda and a sadistic, torture-loving lieutenant, after which Kenton reflects on the other side of politics that a correspondent/journalist rarely sees:

> It was difficult, Kenton had found, to spend any length of time in the arena of foreign politics without perceiving that political ideologies had very little to do with the ebb and flow of international relations. It was the power of Business, not the deliberations of statesmen, that shaped the destinies of nations. The Foreign Ministers of the great powers might make the actual declarations of their Governments' policies; but it was the Big Business men, the bankers and their dependents, the arms manufacturers, the oil companies, the industrialists, who determined what those policies should be. Big Business asked the questions that it wanted to ask when and how it suited it. Big Business also provided the answers. (78)

With his recent game of pokerdice in mind, Kenton concludes his meditation by reformulating the metaphor: "The Big Business man was only one player in the game of international politics, but he was the player who made all the rules" (79).

Ambler's invective against international capitalism is less significant for the light it throws on the hypocrisy of the so-called legitimate workings of business and geopolitics than for the more subtle beam it casts on the other end of the dealings from the boardroom. Ambler's instinct is to seek out dingy barrooms and smoke-filled offices near the waterfront or the *souk;* his deep intuition is to investigate the "psychoneuroses and violence" in the dead-end alleys of some grimy Balkan maze or Middle Eastern hill town. His foray into the low end of big business dealings is microcosmic, focusing on the murky moral landscape of the individual who actually does the dirty work.

Throughout his career, Ambler has been fascinated by the titanic events wrought by the hapless loner or the vindictive psychopath, but the result is identical: history can be, and is, changed frequently by the minuscule or the accidental. The same can be said for innocent protagonists who are transformed from hunted to hunter: ideology is nearly incidental to the emergent and universal helplessness of the survivor. As Gavin Lambert says so succinctly of this Ambler ambiguity: "Although the Marxian argument reflects the intellectual left-wing climate of his time, Ambler uses it to convey a very un-Marxian feeling of personal helplessness" (108). This focus on the microcosmic "dirty little war" of espionage was a great discovery for Ambler—and the entire genre; but Ambler never fulfilled the potential of this theme and subject. This lack of ideology becomes the necessary ingredient of the cold war formula, later developed at midcentury by Le Carré and Deighton. Ambler preferred a normal war's "eve of destruction" formula, most likely because it was his own "background to danger" as he went to World War II and possibly because of the technological clairvoyance that was afforded him by his engineer's training. Finally, his own fascination with the complex political theory of the 1920s was probably too well-rooted to give way to political pessimism; that awaited him in the 1950s.

More than his experience with the Hyde Park Sunday soapbox speaker or the introduction to Communist party leader Raymond Swingler (both reported in *Here Lies*), Ambler's choice of nightly reading of George Gissing during this period must also be viewed as a source of his attraction to the literary use of politics and economics as dual themes. In novels such as *Workers in the Dawn* and *New Grub Street,* Gissing illustrated the injustices of a whole system of society that kept the lower classes in ghastly conditions. Gissing's socialism was never as well-developed as

William Morris's or Bernard Shaw's, but his youthful and genuine enthusiasm was deeply grounded in radical politics and religious agnosticism—two features eminently appealing to the bright, young engineering apprentice from southeast London. Irving Howe said of Gissing: "His single greatest power lies in depicting the life of educated and partly educated persons who are rootless and unhappy precisely to the extent that they have managed to lift themselves out of a lower-class environment and approach the precincts of cultivation. . . . This alienated figure . . . will soon be appearing everywhere in modern literature."[10]

This theme, rooted in Gissing's undercurrent skepticism, must have been enormously attractive to Ambler. His own ambivalence toward science and learning, sustained by his lifelong opposition to elitism in all forms, surely found an early sponsor and model in Gissing. Despite Ambler's relentless assault on international capitalism in *Background to Danger,* he never became fully affiliated with the party because of his loathing for the "academic" language and the atmosphere of elitism. The literary sources of his so-called "left-wing politics" exerted much more influence than the party itself.

Gissing and George Moore (Ambler was particularly impressed by *Esther Waters*) are to be seen in one final perspective in *Background to Danger.* The fin de siècle British realists exerted considerable influence on a generation of postrealist writers (just as the American writers Upton Sinclair and John Dos Passos did on the American side of the Atlantic) who carried the sentiments of quasi-socialism into the collectivist 1930s. The development of a realistic style, as noted by the critics, on the part of Ambler in his second novel seems to involve a technique found in Gissing, and even in Thomas Hardy. Irving Howe describes the stylistic device aptly: "Somewhat like Hardy, [Gissing] . . . commands in *New Grub Street* a notable gift for symbolic condensation through fragments of incident, bits and pieces of action, that seem to contain the meaning of the book in a few words or gestures" (xx). (Interestingly enough, "condensation" was also a device [along with "transfer"] explored by Jung as part of the instrumentation of the "collective unconscious" in its construction of archetypal symbols.[11])

Ambler had begun to utilize this stylistic technique in associations of the "tobacco pipe of tranquillity" in *The Dark Frontier.* The pokerdice game in *Background to Danger* serves as the enduring and final symbol of the elements of change and manipulation in that novel's condemnation of the higher-stakes game of big business and war. *Background to Danger* concludes in the manner of several Ambler novels—with the hero on a train journey that will presumably return him to his accustomed life of normalcy. The final return is, of course, always an impossible journey. Kenton, at the end of his foray into danger and intrigue, boards a train for Berlin in the Prague station, and as the train pulls out, three traveling salesman invite him to a game of pokerdice. Kenton's response—the final words of the novel—are: "Thank you, *mein Herr.* It is good of you. I am afraid I don't play" (245). Kenton, who has witnessed the real stakes of international commerce, knows with a deep conviction that the alleged maximum stake of one pfennig is the fragile crust on a monstrous series of involvements in which innocent appearances belie a harrowing reality. That reality is given a new camouflage in the very beginning of the next novel, *Epitaph for a Spy.*

Epitaph for a Spy

The third of Ambler's novels, *Epitaph for a Spy* (1938), opens with Josef Vadassy's arrival at the French Riviera resort, Hotel de la Réserve, in St. Gatien. Vadassy, a teacher of languages, is at the end of his summer vacation, and he is due back in Paris at the language school in a few days. He is also a man without a country; his personal history as a Hungarian ethnic working in Paris without valid papers is a reflection of the Eastern European turmoil in the years between the wars. To read Eric Ambler in the mid-1990s is to remember the violent and perpetually shifting hegemonies of the Balkans before the relative calm of the nearly fifty-year *Pax Russiana* after World War II. To observe the atrocities in former Yugoslavia in the mid-1990s is to appreciate Ambler's view that danger and violence are always closer at hand than they appear.

This view is quickly imposed on the language teacher. On his second day at the resort, Vadassy is arrested and brought to the police station to face charges of espionage growing out of the fact that he, an amateur photographer, is the owner of film showing a series of shots of the French coastal artillery. He pleads ignorance of the photos, but the *commissaire* finds his innocence impossible to believe. Vadassy is a nature photographer with a penchant for studies in unusual designs and shadows; his favorite subjects are the lizards of the Riviera. Before his arrest, Vadassy observes a lizard darting into the shade of the terrace:

> Its tail lay curved in a neat semicircle, making a tangent of the diagonal division between the tiles. Lizards have an uncanny sense of design.
>
> It was this lizard which reminded me of my photographs.[12]

This confluence of camouflage, *chiaroscuro* (the artistic contrast of light and dark), and the motif of the "serpent in the Garden of Eden" prefigures the imminent danger and fall of the natural, stateless man, Vadassy. In a matter of hours, at the time of his arrest and being charged as a spy, Vadassy will learn even more about photography and the "uncanny sense of design" in the dark shadows of even the brightly lit playpen of the French Riviera. The police find that they can make only one charge against him stick; to clear himself, Vadassy agrees to work with them to find the real culprit. He then becomes both hunter and hunted in an elaborate maze of complications as he must, in order to preserve his freedom and life of normalcy, unravel an intricate web of accident and design. From a list of ten guests and two hotel managers, he must ferret out the real spy. The Hotel de la Réserve becomes a labyrinth of "uncanny design" with its strange array of guests with their many nationalities, languages, and personalities.

One of the most conspicuous (and, of course, suspicious) guests is a German national from Berlin, Herr Emil Schimler, who passes his time at the resort by playing billiards and reading Nietzsche. As a German traveling under an alias, he becomes a prime suspect. Ambler, of course, would have the reader suspect an ulterior motive in Schimler, with Nazi Germany flexing its muscle toward the Mediterranean at the time, and he has Vadassy ask incredulously, "[Did] spies quote Hegel? Did they read Nietzsche?" and then proceed to a sequence of logic and ambiguity: "'Why shouldn't they?' What did it matter, anyway? One might just as well ask: 'Do spies make good husbands?' 'Why shouldn't they?' Why not, indeed?" (64). Ambler not only plays with the notion of camouflage here but with the motif of Everyman as spy—the propinquity of hazard and the thin protection of social order are pervasive Ambler themes.

Herr Schimler is also a more developed portrait of the Nietzschean philosopher, and by extension reflects Ambler's caricature of contemporary Nazi Germany. At one point, during a game of billiards that is really a game of cat and mouse between Schimler and Vadassy, the German asks, "Do you know Germany well, Herr Vadassy? . . . You should go. The people are so nice" (64). Vadassy avoids a direct answer, but realizes there was no question at all. Earlier in this dialogue, Schimler revealed himself to be a Nietzschean turned Hegelian:

> "Nietzsche *might* have been a great man." He flicked the book [*The Birth of Tragedy*] lying on his knees with his forefinger. "This is his earliest work

> and there are seeds of greatness in it. Fancy diagnosing Socrates as a decadent. Morality as a symptom of decadence! What a conception. But what do you think he wrote about it about twenty years later? . . ."
>
> "He said that it smelt shockingly Hegelian. And he was quite right. Identity is the definition only of a simple, immediate, dead thing, but contradiction is the root of all movement and vitality. Only in so far as a thing has in itself contradiction does it move, does it possess an impulse and activity. . . . What the young Nietzsche perceived with Hegel, the old Nietzsche despised. The old Nietzsche went mad." (62)

Herr Schimler then invites Vadassy to a game of Russian billiards. Ambler's symbolism is not lost, not even in the novel's welter of nineteenth-century political theory. Schimler has converted from social democracy to communism; and the puzzle for Vadassy is which enemy—Nazi or Communist—is interested in the coastal fortifications of the French Navy? Furthermore, like the lizards, Schimler's expert and "uncanny sense of design" propels his vigorous billiards game of angles and symmetry; like the lizard, or the chameleon, the idea of a philosopher-spy, fortified by the Nietzschean slogans of "impulse and vitality," suggests a new scale of upheaval and change. For Ambler, the world of 1938 was one committed to more than one course of self-destruction.

Much later in his nearly futile pursuit of the spy in the house of pleasure, Vadassy contemplates the twentieth-century dislocations condensed in the microcosmic hotel:

> It would be good now, I thought, to be in Paris. The afternoon city heat would have gone. It would be good to sit under the trees in the Luxembourg, the trees near the marionette theatre. It would be quiet there now. There would be no one there but a student or two reading. There you could listen to the rustle of leaves unconscious of the pains of humanity in labor, of a civilization hastening to destruction. There, away from this brassy sea and blood-red earth, you could contemplate the twentieth-century tragedy unmoved; unmoved except by pity for mankind fighting to save itself from the primeval ooze that welled from its own subconscious being. (140)

The contrapuntal images of birth and death are reminiscent of Schimler's fondness for Nietzsche's *The Birth of Tragedy.* As a stateless individual, Vadassy is positioned for the macrocosmic perspective that all nations and allegiances require an ideology; and, ultimately, it was a credo-less form of energy—conflict of all oppositions—that would produce change and perhaps apocalyptic destruction. Vadassy contributes the echoes of

Jung and Spengler to the Nietzschean articulations: as a student of Nietzsche, Spengler described the decline of civilization; in addition, Ambler's twofold use of the notion of the "unconscious" in this passage betrays his Jungian underpinnings, in the analogue between the individual psyche and the "collective unconscious." Ambler's analogy is a curious one: just as analytical psychology had revealed a many-layered individual psyche, so did a society (or perhaps a "civilization" in the 1930s conception of Arnold Toynbee) have corresponding strata of civilized to savage stages. But Vadassy quite clearly enunciates a theory of "cultural evolution" based on the Jungian premise of the "collective unconscious" that spawns common evolutionary paths, proven by the existence of archetypes, in diverse civilizations.

In this admixture of political and social philosophies, Ambler quite simply states that civilizations, like all life forms, have a life and death cycle. Struggle and violence are the midwives to the birth and pallbearers for the death. Vadassy's contemplative detachment adds the putative perspective of thought divorced from action; Vadassy is the forerunner of the writer, Latimer, in Ambler's *A Coffin for Dimitrios,* who comes to the realization that the power of the intellect (as found in logic and the arts) is helpless in the face of action and energy on the scale of cosmic oppositional forces. The ancient Heraclitean aphorism "All is in flux" is recapitulated in the combined and modern predictions of Nietzsche and Hegel; Ambler finds further validation in the discoveries of Jung and the pronouncements of Spengler. In the late 1930s prewar years, Ambler intuited accurately that the world was making a mad dash toward a wrenching cataclysm. He employed the forces of modern philosophy and social science to bolster those prefigurings. Ambler will articulate these views most fully in his last two of the prewar novels, *A Coffin for Dimitrios* and *Journey into Fear* (discussed in chapter 4).

As Ambler notes in *Here Lies, Epitaph for a Spy* was not picked up by Knopf in 1938 (135). When the novel was finally published by Knopf in 1951, Ambler wrote a "Footnote" (epilogue) for the American edition, in which he makes his famous statement: "In most human beings ideas of spying and being spied upon touch the fantasy system at deep and sensitive levels of the mind" (200). Even some thirteen years after the writing of the novel, Ambler's use of Jungian notions and language reveals his most abiding response to his prewar narrative of a "civilization hastening to destruction." Both individuals and whole societies were struggling to save themselves from "the primeval ooze that welled from its own subconscious being."

Ambler's wrong-man protagonists are unwitting witnesses, spies, who maintain the reserve of rational consciousness against the onslaught of unconscious elements. Ambler heroes are, in Nietzschean terms, Apollonian survivors in the first skirmishes against the revenant Dionysiac Furies. In *Epitaph for a Spy,* the Hotel de la Réserve is one of the last Victorian houses of crime and detection. The reptilian, shadowy world of ambiguity and design suggests a level of danger akin to that invasive "primeval ooze," in which the *reserve* of reason is threatened with extinction.

Cause for Alarm

Cause for Alarm (1938) also heralds the imminent conflagration of world war and is Ambler's most explicit in naming the Axis powers—Germany and Italy—as insidious incendiary devices. Ironically, the "cause for alarm" is not the alliance of the Axis countries but their mutual distrust. In the words of the genial and helpful Soviet agent, Zaleshoff (first seen in *Background to Danger*), "Have you ever watched a cat and a dog lie down on the same floor?"[13] The two animals can never quite forget the undercurrent of suspicion between them. Such is the dangerous friendship of Germany and Italy.

Into this dangerous liaison steps British engineer Nicholas Marlow, who inadvertently becomes the object of recruitment by both sides. Of Marlow's predicament, Lambert states: "Like all of Ambler's best work this novel is about a rite of passage" (109). Marlow's passage includes two dark crossings: the first is the initiation into the moral questions of conducting big business at the international level (the first half of the novel); the second is the arduous night journey across the mountains into Yugoslavia (the second half). In both passages Marlow loses an earlier innocence that seems irretrievable when he returns home to an England somnolently reposing in a depression and a "phony war."

Marlow, who travels to Milan as an engineer for Spartacus Machine Tool of England, is going to work for a company that will manufacture shell casings for the Italian government. From Ambler's point of view, the real business at hand, as Marlow gets initiated into the bigger businesses of war and espionage, is the cash-nexus between business, politics, and war machines. Ultimately, he becomes submerged in the epistemological questions.

At the intersection of Italian Fascist police, Italian secret service, a German agent (a mysterious Yugoslav General Vagas who loves the ballet), and the friendly Soviet Zaleshoff is a bewildered English engineer who discovers rather quickly that his predecessor was murdered and that the office files are replete with mysterious memoranda of transactions never reported to London. It is Zaleshoff who informs Marlow of the nature of the nasty little game in town: "That's Vagas' job—checking up. If the Italians tell their Nazi boy friends that they're building *two* hundred and fifty new-type bombing planes this year, Uncle Vagas gets busy and checks up to make sure that it isn't *five* hundred and fifty. Dictators who can't even trust their own subordinates out of their sight aren't likely to trust each other very far" (106).

Surrounded by camouflaged ideologues, Marlow is forced to save himself from the spies by becoming a spy himself. He holds the naive belief that he can maintain a neutrality in his dangerous environment (like England itself?) without incurring any of the risks of making that welter of conflict and ideology even more dangerous through the manufacture and sale of weapons. Marlow protests his foolish neutrality to the savvy and unctuous General Vagas: "I am concerned with selling machine tools. I am merely the agent. I did not create the situation. . . . There is a job to be done. If I do not do it, then someone else will" (78). Marlow's simplicity is as fragile, and as hazardous, as the alliance of the Axis powers. Marlow might know the engineering of ballistics, but his rite of passage is the initiation into the knowledge of human nature and praxis: the human factors of hatred and violence that accompany the deployment of arms and political action.

Marlow is the modern technological man who can no longer claim a neutrality for merely possessing the instruments of life and death; he must come to terms with the existential realities—weapons are not made for some sterile zone of human activity. Weapons, and ideas, are always connected to some path of activity, and, according to Nietzsche, it is *action* above all else that binds the individual to existence. Or in this case of weapons of mass destruction, the reality might be nonexistence.

As Marlow discovers a world of imminent danger and violence, he also learns of the secret source of vitality at its center: "Vagas might talk glibly about necessary intelligence, routine precautions and private business arrangements; but that was merely a polite way of putting it. The word was 'espionage.' . . . It all seemed unreal, part of another world, it did not touch your own everyday life at any point. Yet this world of spies and counterspies did exist. Spies had to live somewhere. They had their work to do like anyone else" (83). Like Barstow the physicist, Marlow finds that his scientific training in the observable physical data of the universe's appearances is precious little preparation for discovering the hidden realities of human nature.

In this regard, Ambler provides the reader once again with a Jungian clue early in the novel. The hint was also being supplied to Marlow by the crafty General Vagas, but the foreshadowing in the language of analytical psychology is lost on the trained engineer. Vagas, who first comes to visit Marlow wearing a masklike rouge with a touch of the grotesque, instructs Marlow in the area of appearances versus reality: "It is, I think, impossible to know any man. His thoughts, his own secret emotions, the way his mind works upon the things he sees—those things are the man. All that the outsider sees is the shell, the mask—you understand? Only sometimes do we see a man and then . . . it is through the eyes of an artist" (34). Ambler will return to this Jungian notion of the "mask" in his next novel, but for now the education of Nicky Marlow involves Jung, Nietzsche, and the heart of ideological darkness.

In the final analysis, *Cause for Alarm* posits the central ideological opposition of the period in the juxtaposition of General Vagas (the Nietzschean, and by extension the national socialist) and General Zaleshoff (the Marxian socialist). Vagas's unswerving allegiance is to Germany, and, indirectly, to the philosophy put forth by Nietzsche in *The Birth of Tragedy.* When Vagas invites Marlow out to an evening of ballet at Milan's La Scala, Vagas is given one of the novel's finest and most frightening speeches:

> [T]he ballet interests me enormously. It is, I believe, the final expression of a disintegrating society. The idea of the dance, you know, and the preparation for death have been inseparable since the human animal first crept through the primeval forest. Ballet is merely a new rationalisation of society's instinctive movement towards self-destruction. A dance of death for the Gadarene swine. It has always been so. . . . If I never read a newspaper, Mr. Marlow, one evening at the ballet would tell me that once again society is preparing for death. (75)

This Dionysiac message about the necessary destruction of the Apollonian world of beautiful appearances by strenuous and violent forces comes with a trenchant clarity from Nietzsche—and is delivered without a trace of sarcasm in the balconies of the classically structured La Scala. There is a full examination of Ambler's use of Nietzsche's philosophy in chapter 4; for now let suffice a brief synopsis from *The Birth of Tragedy* of Nietzsche's comments on dance and opera. There Nietzsche attempted to explain Greek tragedy through a modern equivalent, grand opera. He avers that

the ancient drama originated in an epoch of whole person and holistic action: it was a poetic drama that employed painting, architecture, song, dance, and music. Tragedy was the Dionysiac product of instinct; opera is Apollonian and a product of the visionary and ephemeral. Ancient drama originated in the religious impulse to pay homage to the mystery; modern opera and all baroque art pay tribute to the Apollonian notion of empty space. In fact, on this last point, Oswald Spengler, the Nietzschean disciple, had a great deal to say in *The Decline of the West.* Ambler's sources for the posturing elitism of the social nationalism of General Vagas lie in these texts.[14]

The antipode of Vagas is the benevolent and life-saving General Zaleshoff. Actually reared in America, Zaleshoff laces his mild Marxism with a Chicago vernacular; Ambler suggests that the Soviet general is the closest thing to home for a Briton in a desperate situation. In the company of Zaleshoff, Marlow makes a mad dash for life through the wintry passes of the Dolomite mountains into a sanctuarial Yugoslavia. In fact, the camaraderie (or should we say Komradship?) between Marlow and the Soviet spy is viewed by Bernard Bergonzi, in his 1986 study *The Myth of Modernism and Twentieth Century Literature,* as a touchstone of "the intellectual commitment to the Soviet system" on the part of the British intelligentsia of the 1930s. To underscore the appeal of Soviet socialism, Bergonzi uses Ambler's *Cause for Alarm* as a literary exemplum for his "alarming" observation: "We now know that a number—just how many remains uncertain—of well-bred and well-educated young Englishmen began as socialists and ended as Soviet agents."[15] Bergonzi should have the final word on Ambler's fourth prewar novel: "Ambler's novel remains . . . a curious memento of a particular phase of historical consciousness in the late thirties; it presents an abortive myth—the tough, genial, omnicompetent Soviet agent saving the muddled Westerner—that did not survive the history of the next few years. Zaleshoff is a figure from Soviet self-mythologizing briefly transposed into a Western literary context" (125).

Soviet socialism would survive the struggles of the 1930s and 1940s and persist for at least another fifty years after the publication of this novel; but first Ambler was to more precisely foretell the Nietzschean catastrophe of World War II.

Chapter Four
The Eternal Return: Dionysus as Dimitrios

At a pivotal moment in Eric Ambler's third novel, *Epitaph for a Spy,* Vadassy realizes he must engage in espionage to redeem himself. Already the accidental victim of the unknown agent's mistake, the teacher of languages must "bridge the gulf between thought and action"; with Vadassy having already been lectured on Nietzsche by the prime suspect, Herr Schimler, the irony of being forced into a dangerous mode of action is lost on neither Vadassy nor the reader. Perhaps this is the moment in the novel Ambler was thinking of years later when he wrote, "In most human beings ideas of spying and being spied upon touch the fantasy system at deep and sensitive levels of the mind."

Vadassy vacillates as he ponders the literal and figurative portal through which he is resigned to pass: "It is easy to contemplate searching someone's room—standing before the mirror I had had no qualms—but when it comes to the mechanics of the business, the actual entry into the room, it is far from easy. It is not merely the fear of discovery that deters. It is the sense of privacy that is violated. There is a strange door, a strange door-handle and, beyond it, part of another person's life. To open the door seems as inexcusable an intrusion as spying on a pair of lovers" (*Epitaph,* 122). Vadassy's voyeuristic correlative oddly summons up a Freudian fantasy of sexual love; but, as Ambler reminds us, his preferences run more to Jung than to Freud (and perhaps this partly explains the near-total absence of sexuality in Ambler's novels).[1]

Rather than opening to a room of intimacy, the door in the quintessential Ambler novel opens to sudden death and inescapable danger. Ambler explores the many faces of Thanatos—the death instinct—instead of the associations between Eros and espionage later explored by such writers as Ian Fleming and John Le Carré. The faces of Thanatos wear several Jungian masks, or personae; and in Ambler's next (and perhaps finest) novel the innocent Latimer strays through the door to witness death and—under the title published in England in 1939—*The Mask of Dimitrios.*

A Coffin for Dimitrios

Published as *A Coffin for Dimitrios* in the United States (also in 1939),[2] Ambler's fifth novel has emerged as a pivotal one for both Ambler and the genre of the popular thriller because of two ingredients: its peculiar style and its substance. The novel represents one of those high-water marks from which a view both backward and forward is offered. In the matter of substance, the novel looks back to the detective formula. *Dimitrios* is essentially a novel of detection, and the protagonist is a writer of mystery fiction. But the novel metamorphoses in the act of reading, as it did perhaps in the act of writing for Ambler.

From the chrysalis of the Victorian crime novel emerges the novel of espionage and international intrigue. The subjects are crime and the main character's "experiment in detection." But in the very existential act of applying the techniques of deductive reasoning and the science of investigation, the putative detective discovers the limits of the process. The methodical investigator reaches the outer boundaries of his art and science; and in this swift discovery of the defeat of detection lies the even more menacing delimitation of reason itself. One of Ambler's great achievements in *Dimitrios* is to acknowledge new forces and powers that stump and mystify traditional human intellect and its rational faculties. Ambler has chronicled the end of that Victorian and Edwardian social construction found in the detective novel of manners. By the end of *Dimitrios,* even the detective/writer longs for the world that has evanesced: he dreams of a return to the ideal crime scene—"an English country village" where there are "garden parties at the vicarage" and the obligatory clink of teacups. He knows such a place no longer exists.

The second salient feature of *Dimitrios* is the narrative style and technique—a series of third-party narratives on many levels, looking ahead to the storytelling techniques of John Le Carré, who constructs a legendary and secret world about spies who investigate spies. In Le Carré, and certainly in Ambler, the ultimate spy is the reader, whose assemblage of information and narrative must give the tale its final meaning.

A Coffin for Dimitrios builds up a powerful crescendo of suspense when Charles Latimer, a British professor of political economy and well-known author of detective stories, becomes engrossed in the search for the true identity of a man known as Dimitrios. Latimer learns of the existence of Dimitrios by chance. At a party in Istanbul, Latimer is introduced to Colonel Haki. Latimer does not know that Colonel Haki is the chief of Turkish secret police—a soldier of fortune turned intelligence chief.

Haki's intentions are benign; he has admired Latimer's detective stories and proposes a plot for a novel to Latimer. So far the shadow of Somerset Maugham's Colonel R and the reluctant enlistment in *Ashenden* hangs heavy in the air. But the world of Eric Ambler is replete with chance and the dispassionate timing of the blind gods. Latimer happens to be in Haki's office when the police chief is informed of the discovery of the corpse of Dimitrios the Greek, a known murderer. This chance discovery sends Latimer on an odyssey across Europe toward a confrontation with death.

Haki—who enjoys what he calls "romans policier"—and Latimer had been discussing the nature of murder when the report of Dimitrios's death arrives. Haki initiates Latimer's quest when he asks: "I wonder if you are interested in *real* murderers, Mr. Latimer" (10). Art, Haki implies, is never a substitute for real-life encounters with death, espionage, and experience itself:

> "I find the murderer in a *romans policier* much more sympathetic than a real murderer. In a *romans policier* there is a corpse, a number of suspects, a detective and a gallows. That is artistic. The real murderer is not artistic. I, who am a sort of policeman, tell you that squarely." He tapped the folder on his desk. "Here is a real murderer. We have known of his existence for nearly twenty years. This is his dossier. We know of one murder he may have committed. There are doubtless others of which we, at any rate, know nothing. This man is typical. A dirty type, common, cowardly, scum. Murder, espionage, drugs—that is the history. There were also two affairs of assassination." (11)

The opposition of art and reality is sustained throughout the novel, and Latimer's close brush with death grows out of his momentary movement from the aseptic and tidy ideology of academic murder in fiction to the unruly, chaotic world of smokey bistros where actual murder and assassination are plotted. In short, Latimer progresses from observer to participant, and finds that the neat ground rules in the detective's process of deduction are ineffectual in the face of brutal reality.

A philosophy of history is always as important in an Ambler novel as the social context in which the novel is written—one complements the other. *A Coffin for Dimitrios* was written in 1939, on the eve of World War II. Ambler's particular philosophy of history reflects his readings of Nietzsche and Spengler (to be discussed later), along with the concurrent opinion that Europe (and Western civilization) had reached a stage of decadence where an inevitable self-destruction was necessary. The articulation of this philosophy of history is usually reserved for Ambler's villains, although a residual ambiguity always seems to infect the surviving protagonists, insofar as they are left to ponder the nature of civilization and its shadowy discontents. One of the minor ironies of the novel consists in the fact that Latimer, aside from writing detective fiction, is a lecturer in political economy at a minor English university (the quintessential nexus of vicarage and garden); yet when he moves from his secure sphere of observation out to the role of participant in actual melodrama, he learns a lesson in both politics and economics. Or, more precisely he learns that the realms of politics and economics are where good and evil meet. Ambler writes in this significant passage (also cited in chapter 2): "Dimitrios was not evil. He was logical and consistent; as logical and consistent in the European jungle as the poison gas called Lewisite and the shattered bodies of children killed in the bombardment of an open town. The logic of [Michelangelo's] *David,* Beethoven's quartets and Einstein's physics had been replaced by that of the *Stock Exchange Year Book* and Hitler's *Mein Kampf*" (174–75).

In a landmark 1968 essay on Eric Ambler and the spy story, Julian Symons comments on this section of *Dimitrios.* Symons extrapolates the meanings of Ambler's key passage on the connection between Dimitrios and modern history, explaining, somewhat in the fashion of Spengler on the nature of the baroque, that *David* in Michelangelo encapsulated all of the cosmic harmony of the spheres that bespoke a deep faith in providence. Beethoven composed his quartets amid the erosion of belief in the providential theory of history and at a time when other systematic explanations were already competing for favor. Symons cites the Napoléonic (and later Nietzschean and Hitlerian) declaration that fate had been replaced by politics.[3]

In the course of the nineteenth century, new scientific and positivistic systems offered more appealing and practical explanations for the haphazard facts of the universe. Meanwhile, theories of evolution and psychotherapy emerged in popular polemic to rout the belief that God's intervention and order were the mainsprings of history. In this atmosphere of belief in the visible and the physical, Einstein formulated a system of "relativity"—where everything is changeable. Einstein, in fact, passed beyond the physics of Newton into a realm of metaphysics. The beauty of Einstein's theory was that it retained enough of the old mysticism to still consider the presence of a "providence" in history. Nevertheless, the notions that civilization should reach such a final period of corruption and that a man such as Dimitrios should embody the very spirit of the age are equally as "logical and consistent" in their grotesqueness. Hitler and Dimitrios had won out over Beethoven and Einstein. Europe was finally to be reduced to its primordial jungle-state by poison gas and bombardment. Ambler's judgment about Europe in 1939 is quite unmistakable.

Equally unmistakable is Ambler's debt to Nietzsche and Spengler. Latimer's obsession with the history of the criminal and psychopathic Dimitrios begins with the individual but must necessarily conclude with a lesson in the history of the epoch. Latimer's quest begins: "I suddenly had a curious desire to know more about Dimitrios. . . . I wanted to explain Dimitrios, to account for him, to understand his mind. Merely to label him with disapproval was not enough. I saw him not as a corpse in a mortuary but as a man, not as an isolate, a phenomenon, but as a unit in a disintegrating social system" (56–57). Near the end of his journey of investigation, after many horrible eyewitness accounts and revelations about the nature of Dimitrios, Latimer arrives at a morally relativistic position while he contemplates his quarry in a Paris hotel room across the river from the darkened Louvre: "If there *were* such a thing as Evil, then this man . . . But it was useless to try to explain him in terms of Good and Evil. They were no more than baroque abstractions" (174).

Dimitrios is the embodiment of Nietzsche's idea of being "beyond good and evil," as expressed in his volume with that title. Against the darkened backdrop of the Louvre, Latimer's effete means of apprehending, literally and figuratively, someone of the nature of Dimitrios is momentarily poised in the Nietzschean oppositions of Apollonian and Dionysiac. The Louvre is a collection of cultural relics from a dead Apollonian past; Dimitrios is the Dionysiac avatar of a new age, replete with Promethean fires of progress and destruction. Ambler's knowledge of Nietzsche and the notion of "beyond good and evil" contribute to the thoughts that lead Latimer to connect the rise of Dimitrios to the collapse of Western art and culture. The Nietzschean philosophy, which Ambler drew from so frequently in the writing of six prewar novels, is worth a brief examination.

Beyond Good and Evil was the book that Nietzsche used to elucidate his earlier *Thus Spake Zarathustra* and to prepare for the subsequent *The Will to Power.* In the final chapter of *Beyond Good and Evil* Nietzsche posits his doctrine of slave morality and master morality and connects the "aristocracy" of the master morality (or, in the vernacular, a master race) to the Dionysian ideal. This Dionysian model is termed, by

Nietzsche, "the free spirit," and this person cultivates an "unconditioned Will to Power":

> In every country of Europe, and the same in America, there is at present something which makes an abuse of this name [free spirit]: a very narrow, prepossessed, enchained class of spirits, who desire almost the opposite of what our intentions and instincts prompt. . . . What they would fain attain with all their strength, is the universal, green-meadow happiness of the herd, together with security, safety, comfort, and alleviation of life for everyone. . . . We opposite ones, however, who have opened our eye and conscience to the question how and where the plant "man" has hitherto grown most vigorously, believe that this has always taken place under the opposite conditions, that for this end the dangerousness of his situation had to be increased enormously, his inventive faculty and dissembling power (his "spirit") had to develop into subtlety and daring under long oppression and compulsion, and his Will to Life had to be increased to the unconditioned Will to Power:—we believe that severity, violence, slavery, danger in the street and in the heart, secrecy, stoicism, tempter's art and devilry of every kind,—that everything wicked, terrible, tyrannical, predatory, and serpentine in man, serves as well for the elevation of the human species as its opposite.[4]

It would seem that Nietzsche's description of the new Superman, drawn from ancient and unconscious sources of the Dionysiac modes of pure action and existence, beyond the fabricated realm of Apollonian art and morals, is a perfect characterization of the "free spirit" Dimitrios. Nietzsche concludes *Beyond Good and Evil* with the recital of these qualities as the necessary constituents in the moral code of a natural aristocracy of "free spirits." Instead of the Apollonian Vergil as his guide, Latimer is afforded a ghastly vision of hell with the Dionysiac Dimitrios.

It comes as no surprise, then, when Latimer opts to return to the art of detective fiction after his nightmarish adventure in the underworld. Much like the earlier legendary heroes of epic, Latimer begins his quest when he first sees the corpse of Dimitrios. Like Gilgamesh and Odysseus, Latimer visits the House of Death—in his case, the mortuary in Istanbul—and, like those ancient heroes, hopes to apprehend a glimpse of the future from the residents of Hades. Latimer tries to use the life of Dimitrios as a prism in which to read the future:

> Latimer stared at the corpse. So this was Dimitrios. This was the man who had, perhaps, slit the throat of Sholem, the Jew turned Moslem. This

> was the man who had connived at assassinations, who had spied for France. This was the man who had trafficked in drugs, who had given a gun to a Croat terrorist and who, in the end, had himself died by violence. This putty-coloured bulk was the end of an Odyssey. Dimitrios had returned at last to the country whence he had set out so many years before. (19)

Just as Dimitrios comes full circle in his pursuit of violence by meeting a violent death, Latimer returns to his original point of departure: the art of detective fiction. The conclusion of the novel neatly implies that the conflict between art and reality might never be resolved. In the outside world of experience, Latimer had seen brutality and selfishness produce assassination, poison gas, and bombardment—all under the sacrosanct aegis of nationalism and capitalism. Politics and economics—the new theologies—reign supreme; and Dimitrios the Greek had in his own logical way been the incarnate paradigm of the age. Latimer therefore returns to the inner world of art—in particular, detective fiction. The detective story is but an extension of Michelangelo's *David* and Beethoven's quartets—it is the construct emanating from a new harmony of the spheres. It is a world of limited systems, made up of deductively ordered facts. The novel of detection is an enclosed world that is congenial to the refugee from an outer environment of armed hostility and imminent cosmic chaos.

Therefore, when Latimer's philosophical friend, Marukakis, writes a letter in an attempt to explain a man like Dimitrios (one wonders if this is Ambler's own thinly disguised voice), Latimer's reaction is justified. Marukakis/Ambler state:

> As for your Dimitrios: what can one say? A writer of plays once said that there are some situations that one cannot use on the stage; situations in which the audience can feel neither approval nor disapproval, sympathy or antipathy; situations out of which there is no possible way that is not humiliating or distressing and from which there is no truth, however bitter, to be extracted. He was, you may say, one of those unhappy men who are confounded by the difference between the stupid vulgarities of real life and the ideal existence of the imagination. That may be. Yet, I have been wondering if, for once, I do not find myself in sympathy with him. Can one explain Dimitrios or must one turn away disgusted and defeated? I am tempted to find reason and justice in the fact that he died as violently and indecently as he lived. But that is too ingenuous a way out. It does not explain Dimitrios; it only apologises for him. Special sorts of conditions must exist for the creation of the special sort of criminal that

> he typified. I have tried to define those conditions—but unsuccessfully. All I do know is that while might is right, while chaos and anarchy *masquerade* as order and enlightenment, those conditions will obtain. (213–14; italics added)

Latimer misses the reference to the "masque," or the "mask" of Dimitrios, even after his own lengthy dissertation on the obviously Jungian notion of the persona. As Marukakis suggests (in keeping with the title of chapter 14, the source of the British title of the novel), the mask of Dimitrios is one of "order and enlightenment" on the face of what is really "chaos and anarchy." The conditions that allow Dimitrios to flourish are the laws of the jungle—"might is right." The Nietzschean rule of instinct and primal energies heralds the Dionysian triumph of "the will to power"—decorously presented to a modern individual in the masquerade of the Jungian persona. Latimer expostulates at length on the technique of "masking" immediately before coming face to face with the real Dimitrios (who, when he makes his grand entrance, "was a picture of distinguished respectability"). Ambler opens chapter 14, "The Mask of Dimitrios," with a Jungian introduction; it is a personal introduction to the then very much alive Dimitrios:

> A man's features, the bone structure and the tissue which covers it, are the product of a biological process; but his face he creates for himself. It is a statement of his habitual emotional attitude; the attitude which his desires need for their fulfillment and which his fears demand for their protection from prying eyes. He wears it like a devil mask; . . . it is a screen to hide his mind's nakedness. Other men . . . understand instinctively that the mask cannot be the man behind it, they are generally shocked by a demonstration of the fact. The duplicity of others must always be shocking when one is unconscious of one's own. (188)

Thus, Ambler presents the Nietzschean Dionysus in the very language and camouflage of the Jungian persona. As Ambler recalls in his autobiography, "Jung led me to Nietzsche and *The Birth of Tragedy*" (*Here Lies,* 92). That intense reading took place in 1929, in the library at Addiscombe; ten years later, it would be Dimitrios who led Ambler back to both Nietzsche and Jung, via the conduit of Jung's *On the Psychology of the Unconscious.* An examination of the 1916 first edition of that landmark work reveals a connection of theme and image that Ambler would draw upon for the rest of his literary career. In addition, both Nietzsche and Jung had led Ambler to Spengler's *The Decline of the West* (1926), while Jung's preface to his *On the*

Psychology of the Unconscious reveals him to be the link backward to Nietzsche and forward to Spengler. Written during the savage outbreak of World War I, Jung's preface is a primer for the neatly braided elements of subject, theme, and image in Ambler's six prewar novels:

> The psychological accompaniments of the present war . . . are uniquely fitted to force upon the attention of every thinking person the problem of the chaotic unconscious which slumbers uneasily beneath the ordered world of consciousness. This war has pitilessly revealed to civilized man that he is still a barbarian, and has at the same time shown what an iron scourge lies in store for him if ever again he should be tempted to make his neighbour responsible for his own evil qualities. *The psychology of the individual is reflected in the psychology of the nation.* . . . If ever there was a time when self-reflection was the absolutely necessary and only right thing, it is now, in our present catastrophic epoch. Yet whoever reflects upon himself is bound to strike upon *the frontiers of the unconscious,* which contains what above all else he needs to know. (Jung 1956, 12; italics added)

Once again, Jung's use of the frightening theme and the image of "the frontiers of the unconscious" must have impressed the novice Ambler when he constructed the titular image, and multiple meanings, of *The Dark Frontier.* Jung's preface also illuminates the origins of Latimer's obsession with the master spy and criminal Dimitrios. Instead of searching for motive and mechanics of the crimes—those old-fashioned elements of detection and ratiocination—Latimer decides to embark on an "experiment in detection"; the nature of that experiment is disclosed in his first revelation to the journalist, Marukakis: "I wanted to explain Dimitrios, to account for him, *to understand his mind*" (56; italics added). Because of the Jungian pronouncement that the psyche of the individual is connected to the collective psyche of a nation, Latimer discovers his charter to investigate the *mind,* not the motives, of the pathological Dimitrios "as a unit in the disintegrating social system" (57).

This charter, the Jungian postulate of the mask and its roots in the collective unconscious, is lucidly described by Jung in one of the essays Ambler cites as influencing his first novel: "Only by reason of the fact that the persona is a more or less accidental or arbitrary segment of collective psyche can we make the mistake of accepting it *in toto* as something 'individual.' But, as its name shows, it is only a mask for the collective psyche, a mask that *feigns individuality,* and tries to make others and oneself believe that one is individual, whereas one is simply playing a part in which the collective psyche speaks" (Jung 1956, 167). The investigation of the mind of Dimitrios transforms the course of Latimer's life and his outlook; it also transforms the act of detection from the Newtonian and Holmesian world of physics into the Jungian sphere of psychology.

Thus Latimer explains away the biological mask of Dimitrios as the "features of bone structure and tissue" that are something quite different from the psychological mask—that "statement of his habitual emotional attitude" (188). The Jungian mask is the conduit for Latimer's experiment in detection.[5] And, in his essay on "Anima and Animus," Jung states later, "To the degree that the world invites the individual to identify with the mask, he is delivered over to influences from within" (Jung 1956, 205). This is the invisible but unerring path to the individual's own unconscious. The collective unconscious is the dark underworld to which Latimer's experiment leads; like the mythical underworld visitors of ancient epic, he finds a hellish vision of past, present, and future. The "mask of Dimitrios" provides, from the perspective of Latimer's amateurish analytical psychology, a glimpse into the primeval depths of the collective unconscious. Dimitrios also supplies an emphatic demonstration of the results when primitive and frightening forces are funnelled into "the will to power."

Jung addresses "the will to power," and in turn Nietzsche, in one of the sections of *On the Psychology of the Unconscious.* This was the road that led Ambler from Jung to Nietzsche. The complete title of this section is "The Other Point of View: The Will to Power." The implied "first" point of view is the Freudian, comprising the reduction of the basic instincts to Eros and Thanatos, which Jung discusses clearly in an earlier section of the essay, titled "The Eros Theory." Jung dismisses the Freudian fixation on Eros as "questionable" and turns his attention to the Freudian description of the "shadow-side" of man (Jung 1956, 38). Jung follows with a four-page analysis of "instinct"—that formidable dynamism lurking in the background. He then announces that the premiere authority on instinct is not Freud, but Nietzsche (Jung 1956, 40–44).

Jung agrees with Nietzsche that instinct consists of a turbulent, and sometimes demonic, dynamism that constitutes the shadow-side of a human being. Nietzsche called this shadow-side of human nature the Dionysiac; Jung came to describe it as the unconscious. Beyond this basic agreement, Jung enunciates nothing but cautious and critical commentary for the Nietzschean avowal of the impulse to give unquestioning obedience to instinct. Jung poses this question, fraught with danger, in the very year that World War I was devastating Europe: "Has anyone made clear to himself what that means—a yea-saying to instinct? That was what Nietzsche desired and taught, and he was in deadly earnest. With a rare passion he sacrificed himself, his whole life, to the idea of the Superman—to the idea of the man who through obedience to instinct transcends himself" (Jung 1956, 40).

Jung offers the judgment that the ultimate and most deep-seated instinct for Nietzsche is that of self-preservation; it is this very instinct, the will to power, that then nullifies the real possibility of self-transcendence. Jung comments further that this central conflict, and therefore flaw, in the Nietzschean argument also places the Dionysiac impulse in direct conflict with Christian morality (based essentially on self-denial). Nietzsche condemned the Christian suppression of animal nature and attempted to postulate a higher "moral order" beyond good and evil. Jung, who cannot forfeit the protection of institutional religion and its ethical precepts, describes the inevitable failure of some higher realm to prevail. The individual who tries to rise above good and evil, Jung writes, "delivers himself up unresistingly to the animal psyche. That is the moment of Dionysian frenzy, the overwhelming manifestation of the 'blond beast,' which seizes the soul with nameless shudderings. The seizure transforms him into a hero or into a godlike being, a superhuman entity. He rightly feels himself 'six thousand feet beyond good and evil'" (Jung 1956, 42).

The reader who is aware of this Jung-Nietzsche background to Ambler's work here comes to realize that Dimitrios is the latter-day representation of that Jungian depiction of the "blond beast"—the Aryan Superman prefigured here and even earlier in the Nietzschean espousal of an amoral master race of Dionysian "nobility." Again, to cite the very passage in which Ambler characterizes Dimitrios in terms of being outside of good and evil: "But it was useless to explain him in terms of Good and Evil. They were no more than baroque abstractions [hence, Apollonian forms]. Good business and Bad Business were the elements of the new theology [thus, Christianity is dead]. Dimitrios was not evil. He was logical and consistent; as logical and consistent in the European jungle as the poison gas. . . . The logic of [Michelangelo] . . . Beethoven . . . and Einstein had been replaced by that of the *Stock Exchange Year Book* and Hitler's *Mein Kampf*" (174–75).

Compare Ambler's rhetoric and his theme in this last passage with that of Jung's final thoughts on Nietzsche: "A life like Nietzsche's, lived to its fatal end with rare *consistency* to the nature of the underlying instinct for power, cannot simply be explained away as bogus" (Jung 1956, 43; italics added). For Jung, and later for Ambler, the explanation lies in the understanding of the Faustian tragedy, in what it means to accept instinct and its weird unconscious world. Jung concludes with an aphoristic lesson: "a man may save himself from the Faustian catastrophe, before which his courage and his strength might well fail him. A whole man, however, knows that his bitterest foe, or indeed a host of enemies, does not equal that one worst adversary, the 'other self' who dwells in his bosom" (Jung 1956, 44).

This glimpse of Dimitrios as the "other self" is the major epiphany of Latimer's "experiment in detection." Much like Oedipus in his search for the patricidal killer, the detective who collides with the unconscious and the instinctive must himself become the quarry. Jung labels this collision as the "identification with the shadow" (Jung 1956, 42), and here precisely lie the origins of the obsession with the shadow of Dimitrios that Latimer bumps into, quite by accident. Latimer is greeted by the shade (or shadow) of Dimitrios in the Istanbul "house of death." Latimer's recoil at the end of the novel represents his profound shock at the moment of recognition in that silent greeting: it is the greeting between old and kindred spirits.

But at that moment of recoil, even as he *misses* the "masque" reference in Marukakis's final letter, Latimer has more important things to think about—he has a novel to finish:

> He needed, and badly, a motive, a neat method of committing a murder and an entertaining crew of suspects. Yes, the suspects must certainly be entertaining. His last book had been a trifle heavy. He must inject a little more humour into this one. As for the motive, money was always, of course, the soundest basis. A pity that Wills and life insurance were so outmoded. Supposing a man murdered an old lady so that his wife should have a private income. It might be worth thinking about. The scene? Well, there was always plenty of fun to be got out of an English country village, wasn't there? The time? Summer; with cricket matches on the village green, garden parties at the vicarage, the clink of tea-cups and the sweet smell of grass on a July evening. That was the sort of thing people liked to hear about. It was the sort of thing that he himself would like to hear about. (214)

Latimer retreats to the inner cosmos of order, sweetness, and light. But as he peers from the train window, "The train ran into a tunnel" (214).

Ambler's final symbolic stroke relinquishes the writer's retreat as an escape of ambiguous efficacy. Which is the twentieth-century man, the child of history: Dimitrios or Latimer?

If Eric Ambler's solution to the dilemma of whether the man of thought or the man of action shapes the progression of history is too obliquely stated in *A Coffin for Dimitrios,* his next novel, *Journey into Fear* (1940), is more explicit. Perhaps Ambler's most critically underrated novel, *Journey into Fear* focuses on the Jungian "blond beast" of Nazi Germany and makes full use of the Spenglerian philosophy of history. In some ways, this last of Ambler's six prewar novels is a sequel to *A Coffin for Dimitrios;* it is the chaotic and lawless arena of conflict bequeathed by the eternal return of Dionysus as Dimitrios.

Journey into Fear

In *Journey into Fear,* a British ballistics engineer is dispatched to Turkey to provide the technical data needed to convert British armaments for Turkish naval vessels. On the night before he is to return to England, a lone gunman attempts to murder him in his Istanbul hotel. It is late 1940, and Allied forces must arm the Turkish vessels before the imminent German spring offensive. Colonel Haki enters the scene, and convinces Mr. Graham, the engineer, to take an Italian steamer back to England. What follows is a "journey into fear."

The Englishman Graham is a devotee of detective stories and one of the top ballistics engineers in the world, but the lessons he learns from his fearful journey come from the pages of Darwin, Jung, Frazer, and Spengler. Like his predecessor, Latimer, Graham comes to find that the deductive processes of the detective and the mathematician are based on systems of harmony and order, nowhere to be found in the grim, grimy game of international espionage and the instinctual drive of self-preservation.

The Italian steamer *Sestri Levante* is a "ship of fools" wherein modern humanity is displayed in a clinical showcase designed by Darwin and Freud (although, as shall presently be discussed, the work of Jung is the real psychology text used). Ambler is extremely effective in bringing the age-old device of a shipboard community of diverse personalities to the espionage genre. In fact, he surpasses Graham Greene's *The Orient Express* in suspense (Anthony Burgess also uses the ship community in his 1966 "eschatological spy novel," *Tremor of Intent*).

Graham receives a smattering of Freud from Colonel Haki's private theory of the psychology of the murderer. Haki gives Graham a word of caution about the Roumanian, Banat, whose mission is to kill Graham: "I have my own theory about men such as Banat. I believe that they are perverts with an *idée fixe* about the father whom they identify not with a virile god . . . but with their own impotence. When they kill, they are thus killing their own weakness. There is no doubt of it, I think" (*Journey,* 52). But Graham is in no frame of mind for abnormal psychology; he is in a state of shock: "Confronted by the proposition that someone was, in fact, not merely hoping for his death but deliberately trying to murder him, he was as profoundly shocked as if he had been presented with incontrovertible proofs that *a* no longer equalled *b* + *c*" (45). The term "proposition" is deliberate, for Graham's world of logical propositions and mathematical equations is about to disintegrate. Like Barstow before him in *The Dark Frontier,* Graham comes to learn of the Ambleresque "weird multiplier."

Once aboard the ship, the thin protection of civilization recedes for Graham. In his stateroom, he reads the following words printed on an old piece of paper from a lifebelt:

> "*In case of danger. . . .*" In case! But you couldn't get away from danger! It was all about you, all the time. You could live in ignorance of it for years: you might go to the end of your days believing that some things couldn't possibly happen to *you,* that death could only come to you with the sweet reason of disease or an "act of God" but it was there just the same, waiting to make nonsense of all your comfortable ideas about your relations with time and chance, ready to remind you—in case you had forgotten—that civilisation was a word and that you still lived in the jungle. (60)

The reality of the Darwinian jungle is ubiquitous, just beneath the surface of appearances. The law of the jungle is also just beneath the surface of a person's skin. Graham is forced to realize the existence of his own survival instincts when he is pressed to obtain a gun and is willing to kill in self-defense. He is also willing to entertain thoughts of a liaison with a Hungarian dancer, and she forces him to recognize his sexual drives, in one of the few Ambler episodes of sexual attraction and amorous activity among his entire pantheon of characters. Ambler indirectly resurrects the Ashenden formula of sex and violence: these two elements are never far removed from the spy genre. But, just as the Freudian formula of sex and violence is rejected by Ambler in his preference for Jung in the transformation of the thriller, the Freudian articulations in this novel are a foil to the more accurate critical light of Nietzsche in the reading of the thematic undercurrent.

Both Colonel Haki and José, the dancer's husband, are ideological ruses. The dancers, José and Josette, may well espouse the Darwinian apothegm of humankind as the "ape in velvet," but their enactment of the Dionysiac dance in a backstreet bistro in Istanbul is a dramatic moment that harkens back to the La Scala opera in Milan in *Cause for Alarm,* when the demonic General Vagas proffers the Nietzschean perspective on dance and death. Brought out for a night's entertainment to Le Jockey Cabaret by the company's Turkish representative, the weary Graham watches the dance of indolent sensuality with the trained eye of the engineer: "it was something to justify the price of the drinks: a demonstration of the fact that, by applying the laws of classical mechanics, one small, unhealthy looking man with a broad sash round his waist could handle an eight stone woman as if she were a child" (13). Instead of laws of physics, Graham should have been on the lookout for the instinctive laws of human nature.

If Graham had been tutored by the wily General Vagas, he might have been prepared for the imminent threat of his own destruction immediately following the dance. But the engineer does not perceive the final warnings, although the reader does. Immediately after the show, Graham is brought backstage by his Turkish escort to meet Josette. She is a sultry tease; as she distractedly entertained her guests, she "had discarded her costume, and put on a rose velvet house-coat" (17). Her husband is nearby, but is willing to barter for his wife's flesh. His favorite axiom is: "Man is an ape in velvet." In the dark Darwinian underworld of Istanbul nightclubs, and later on board the *Sestri Levante* when the dancers show up there also as passengers, the velvet is as thin as the protection of civilization.

Graham initially resists Josette's attempt to seduce him, but soon afterward opens the door onto another kind of danger as he makes the classic transition from quotidian normalcy to the threshold of the jungle. When Graham returns to his hotel room, he opens the Ambleresque door: "He put the key in the lock, turned it, pushed the door open and, with his right hand, felt along the wall for the light switch. The next moment there was a splinter of flame in the darkness and an ear-splitting detonation" 23).

In this sudden encounter with the assassin Graham crosses the threshold; the exact moment is recollected late in the novel as Graham prepares to leave the hazardous "ship of ideological fools" and return to his accustomed life as engineer at Cator and Bliss. As he prepares to go ashore at Genoa and take final leave of Josette, he subconsciously makes the connection that General Vagas might have taught him in the idle moments of watching the dance before he inadvertently entered "the world beyond the door":

> He knew suddenly that it was not Josette of whom he was taking his leave, but of something of himself. In the back streets of his mind a door was slowly closing for the last time. She had complained that for him she was just a part of the journey from Istanbul to London. There was more to it than that. She was part of the world beyond the door: the world into which he had stepped when Banat had fired those three shots at him in the Adler-Palace: the world in which you recognized the ape beneath the velvet. (210)

Little does Graham know, at the point of the attempt on his life, that there are still more doors waiting for him. Whether the doors are the Freudian one of Eros, the Darwinian one of violence, or the Jungian one of instinct and the shadow-side, all of the portals lead to the same path: the subterranean descent to the unconscious. Thus, Ambler's doctrinaire *Journey into Fear* transforms itself into the most complex novel he had written until that time. The novel functions at a level of meaning beyond the dogmatic and intrusive disquisitions of Darwinian or Freudian social science. It takes on a dynamic structure of meaningful relationships that represent the Jungian interplay of the elements of the multilayered psyche. Ambler is a Jungian believer at heart, even though the "mind" of the novel might outwardly and ostensibly be a series of depositions from the emergent social histories of the period (Spengler and Toynbee).

As in previous Ambler novels, the thematic core of the work resides in the philosophy of history. In *Journey into Fear,* the mind of the novel and its philosophy of history are a hybrid of the doctrines of Frazer and Spengler (a world on the eve of destruction), ironically expounded by the chief German agent who is disguised as a German archaeologist. Ambler, writing during the "phony war" of late 1939 and early 1940 (war had been declared, but nothing much was happening), indicates that it is the German nation that has learned the principal Nietzschean lesson of history: might makes right, especially in a transitional epoch. The very same portal to destruction that Graham entered is the one that now awaits the Allies in a world apparently on a course with doom.

Once again, the background for this Ambler novel is a Europe headed for self-destruction, and its history is the cosmic working out of the death and resurrection ritual. Because of its power and will to exercise that power, Ambler warns, through the pronunciations of the German agent, Germany may be the new phoenix to rise from the ashes of Europe's destruction. The German "archaeologist" preaches to the Englishman on the subject of historical destiny: "The scholar in his study can ignore the noise in the market place. Perhaps—if he is a theologian or a biologist or an antiquarian. I am none of those things. I helped in the search for a logic of history. We should have made of the past a mirror from the future. Unfortunately, it no longer matters what we could have seen. We are returning the way we came. Human understanding is re-entering the monastery" (74–75).

The logic of history presented here is the fatalistic and ritualistic theory of a cyclical history as posited by Frazer and Spengler: power is the ruling, fixed principle in an otherwise unstable universe where nations rise and fall. The anthropology of Frazer asserts the waning of Christianity; and the cyclical historicity of Spengler avers the imminent downfall of Western European civilization. Although Ambler specifically cites Spengler as a source for these observations in the novel, nowhere is Frazer mentioned. A possible key to the recognition of Frazer as a source is in Jung; once again, Jung may well have been the conduit for Ambler's exploring a network of modernist intellectual history.

In his 1912 work, *Symbols of Transformation,* Jung makes several references to Frazer's *The Golden Bough* (1890).[6] Jung praises the voluminous work of Frazer for its manifestation of the deep purpose of all of the religious mysteries—they created symbols of death and rebirth. Furthermore, in this monumental essay, Jung often refers to the Gilgamesh epic (an ancient near-Eastern epic from the second millenium B.C.) as an illustration of the dynamic of the will to power. Strangely enough, the Gilgamesh epic is not prominently featured in Frazer; it is cited only sparsely in footnotes. Jung would seem to be the obvious source here of the passage from *Journey into Fear* in which Ambler conflates the famous Frazerian part 4 of *The Golden Bough,* "Dying and the Reviving Gods," with the Jungian inclusions of the Sumerian Gilgamesh and the *Enuma Elish* (creation epic).

The common denominators among these principal exponents of intellectual history who serve as sources for Ambler—Nietzsche, Frazer, and Jung—are twofold: first, that all civilized societies have at some period emerged from a state of savagery that survives in the habits and institutions of the culture; and second, that resemblances between the religions of the East and West point to an unmistakable uniformity of savage and civilized minds that can be explained only by "psychic unity." The Nietzschean eternal return of the Dionysiac became for Frazer the motif in mythology of the "dying god," and *The Golden Bough*'s search for the even more remote comparative types from Sumerian and Middle Eastern antiquity. Eric Ambler became enamored of the quest for the ancient and everlasting sources of the mask of Dimitrios. The return of Dionysus was inevitable—all of the modern weight of anthropology and psychology supported it. And, if those testimonies were not enough, Ambler introduced one more—history itself.

Journey into Fear is a fictional analogue to the historiography of Oswald Spengler. If Spengler's stentorian voice is somewhat muted in Frazerian leanings on the Sumerian pantheon in archaeologist Haller's first speech on the *Sestri Levant,* the influence of the Spenglerian method is irrefutable. Haller unabashedly echoes Spengler's grand design when he says: "I helped in the search for a logic of history" (75). Spengler himself asks in his introduction to *The Decline of the West,* "Is there a logic of history? . . . Is it possible to find in life itself . . . a series of stages which must be traversed . . . in an ordered and obligatory sequence? For everything organic the notions of birth, death, youth, age, lifetime, are fundamentals. . . . In short, is all history founded upon general biographic archetypes?"[7] Thus, it was Spengler who launched the search for a metaphysical logic of history. Spengler's use of the notion of "archetypes" also betrays a knowledge of Jung's *Symbols of Transformation.*

Both Spengler's and Ambler's debts to Jung (in discussion of the power of cultural symbols) comes in this next speech by the disputatious Haller:

> "When you reach my age you sometimes think of the approach of death. I thought this afternoon how much I would have liked to have seen the Parthenon just once more. I doubt if I shall have another opportunity of doing so. I used to spend hours standing in the shade by the Propylaea looking at it and trying to understand the men who built it. I was young then and did not know how difficult it is for Western man to understand the dream-heavy classical soul. They are so far apart. The god of superlative shape has been replaced by the god of superlative force and between the two conceptions there is all space. The destiny idea symbolised by the Doric columns is incomprehensible to the children of Faust. For us . . ." He broke off. (125)

Ambler drew this philosophical statement directly from the pages of Spengler. At the beginning of chapter 5 of *The Decline of the West,* titled "Makrokosmos: Apollinian, Faustian, and Magian Soul," Spengler traces his use of the name "Apollinian" (Spengler's variant spelling) to Nietzsche. In the opening section, which explores the relationships between architecture and divinities, Spengler makes broad distinctions between Apollinian and Faustian souls. The Apollinian soul is represented in classical culture and its anthropomorphic notion of space. The Faustian soul is expressed in the Western culture born in Northern Europe in the tenth century; "its prime symbol is pure and limitless space" (97). For Spengler, the representation of space is a paradigm of cultural symbols that address age-old oppositions between freedom and structure:

> "Space"—speaking now in the Faustian idiom—is a spiritual something, rigidly distinct from the momentary sense-present, which *could* not be represented in an Apollinian language, whether Greek or Latin. But the created *expression-space* of the Apollinian arts is equally alien to ours. In no other Culture is the firm footing, the socket, so emphasized. The Doric column bores into the ground, the vessels are always thought of from below upward, whereas those of the Renaissance float above their footing. (97)

Thus, into the mouth of the Nazi intellectual, Haller, Ambler places the mirrored-speech of the Nietzschean disciple, Spengler. As the spiritual spokesman for nationalist socialism, Haller invokes the Germanic spirits of Goethe and Nietzsche. Ambler creates in this portrait of the archaeologist a pointed illustration of Nazi Germany; it was a country that first had imported not just architectural columns but whole altars, such as the one from Pergamon. Now, with a combined ideology of destiny and infinite space, its Faustian (and Dionysian) spirit would hold sway over an endless domain. In Haller, Ambler constructs not only a sinister henchman but also an "intellectual villain." He is not only the match for the English engineer but also the satin-voiced call of destiny. Not since Sherlock Holmes pursued the brilliant Moriarty had the cerebral detective/spy engaged as attractive an arch-enemy as Graham found in the erudite and self-effacing Haller. But, then again, as Graham would discover, he was observing the mask of Spengler.

By way of Spengler's debt to Jung (he *does* employ the term "archetype" many times in his morphological constructs of a "logic" to history), there appears a curious passage on classical architectural forms in Jung's

1912 introduction to his *Symbols of Transformation.* After inveighing against the "unjustified boldness" of Freud's procedures of analysis in his *Interpretation of Dreams,* Jung credits Freud for grounding his discovery of "individual conflict" in "the monumental drama of the ancient world, the Oedipus legend." Jung then adduces a familiar-sounding analogy:

> The impression made by this simple remark may be likened to the uncanny feeling which would steal over us if, amid the noise and bustle of a modern city street, we were suddenly to come upon an ancient relic—say the Corinthian capital of a long-immured column, or a fragment of an inscription. A moment ago, and we were completely absorbed in the hectic, ephemeral life of the present; then, the next moment, something very remote and strange flashes upon us, which directs our gaze to a different order of things. We turn away from the vast confusion of the present to glimpse the higher continuity of history. Suddenly we remember that on this spot where we now hasten to and fro about our business . . . similar passions moved mankind, and people were just as convinced as we are of the uniqueness of their lives. (Jung 1967, 3)

While one cannot prove the genealogy of the classical architectural column as the guidepost of these early twentieth-century taxonomists of history and the human psyche, Spengler's own indirect acknowledgment of Jung and the very direct naming of Nietzsche are in a section of *The Decline of the West* titled "The Origin of This Book": "Consider . . . the voluminous work that was being done in the domain of folk-psychology on the origins of myths, arts, religions and thought—and done, moreover . . . from a strictly morphological standpoint" (Spengler, 37). With an obvious reference to Freud and Jung, Spengler then credits Nietzsche with the "comprehensive solution"—the recognition of a "world consciousness," the very notion that was described in the new depth psychology as "psychic unity." It was this network of interlocking pieces of a new history and a new philosophy of history that magnetically pulled Ambler from the seemingly sterile world of engineering to a dynamic and robust series of approaches to human nature. There can be little doubt that this knowledge of modern "mass society" contributed to his remarkable success in the nascent ad agency marketplace in the early 1930s. Like his later heroes, Barstow, Marlow, and Graham, Ambler underwent a certain loss of Renaissance innocence as he gazed upon the monstrous and gargantuan shapes of the twentieth century.

Journey into Fear ostensibly constructs a theoretical framework around a simplistic set of oppositions between Graham the engineer and Haller the historian. But the traditional conflict between science and the humanities becomes blurred upon closer inspection; Graham is really a practitioner of the religion of science and Haller is the exponent of a science of religion. Both Graham and Haller, through the instrumentation of Haller's declaiming a new "logic of history," find common intellectual ground in the acceptance of a modern position of relativism. Haller's essential insidiousness as a Nazi agent in disguise lies not only in his plan to murder the British engineer but also, through the indoctrination of his Nietzschean and Spenglerian ideas, in his attempt to destroy the engineer's intellectual conviction.

The ideological conquest is nearly as important for Haller as the homicide. Something more is at stake, Ambler seems to suggest. The doctrine of relativism (right out of Spengler, 181–93) is important in understanding the Nietzschean principle of *tension;* it is that which connects the domains of physics and metaphysics. The Newtonian Graham is forced by the Nietzschean Haller to recognize the impossibility of, in John Dewey's phrase, the quest for certainty. Following Spengler's extrapolation of the dynamic of tension operative in world history, Haller explains to Graham that even scientific truths depend on a religion (Spengler, 188–95) and an epochal relevance. Haller is preparing the fossil world of the Apollonian Graham for the dawning of a new and violent age. For the children of Faust are toying with the ultimate Damoclean sword that hangs above civilization. With the coming technological warfare on a global scale, the offspring of Faust are verging on total annihilation. Haller says:

> Even that which we commonly regard as immortal dies sooner or later. One day the last Titian and the last Beethoven quartet will cease to exist. The canvas and the printed notes may remain if they are carefully preserved but the works themselves will have died with the last eye and ear accessible to their messages. As for the immortal soul, that is an eternal truth and the eternal truths die with the men to whom they were necessary. The eternal truths of the Ptolemaic system were as necessary to the mediaeval theologians as were the eternal truths of Kepler to the theologians of the Reformation and the eternal truths of Darwin to the nineteenth century materialists. The statement of an eternal truth is a prayer to lay a ghost—the ghost of primitive man defending himself against what Spengler calls the "dark almightiness." (154–55)

And when the "dark almightiness" closes in, it is men like Dimitrios and Banat—the traffickers in poison gas and bombs—who eclipse the likes of Titian and Kepler. For Ambler, the reign of the Third Reich's *wermacht,* along with its designs of politics and economics, vitiates and precludes an eternal verity for the twentieth century; it will have justified its own rationale for the will to power, and it is beyond good and evil.

With the abolition of the moral system of good and evil, Haller's real purpose in the intellectual seduction of Graham becomes evident. Haller wishes to offer the British engineer an "opportunity" to support the cause of the future: Nazi Germany. Thus the real theoretical frame of the novel is manifest in a tripartite struggle—Graham is forced to recognize, and react to, the two masks of evil of Nazi Germany. The first was the cold-blooded assassin, Banat; the other, Haller, is even more deadly, the Faustian mind that summons up the monsters from the dark and subterranean world of the mindless and the irrational. What appears to be the dialectic of an ideological conflict between Graham and Haller is actually Ambler's profound dramatization of the more complex and multidimensional Jungian conflict of the individual caught between the conscious and unconscious levels of the psyche. Like his prototype and fellow physicist, Barstow, Graham is Ambler's portrait of a modern and reasonable person who bumps into the Jungian shadow of the unconscious.

The shadow looms up suddenly in the form of Banat, the German agent who bungles the assassination of Graham in the early pages of the novel. Interestingly enough, the failed attempt on Graham's life takes place in his room at the Adler-Palace Hotel. Shortly thereafter, Colonel Haki tries to impress Graham with his knowledge of Freudian analysis. Within the space of a couple of hours, Graham is treated to a smattering of name dropping—Alfred Adler and Freud; but it is the Jungian shadow of Banat that will figure significantly in Ambler's design for the novel's ideological undercarriage. And it is precisely in these terms that Ambler describes the homicidal agent; for Banat, like Dimitrios, is the Dionysiac emissary from the dark unconscious. Watching Banat up close at dinner one evening, Graham wonders whether a jury in an English court of law would find him insane: "Probably not: he killed for money; and the Law did not think that a man who killed for money was insane. And yet he *was* insane. His was the insanity of the sub-conscious mind running naked, of the 'throw back' of the mind which could discover the majesty of God in thunder and lightning, the roar of bombing planes, or the firing of a five-hundred pound shell; the awe-inspired insanity of the primaeval swamp" (126–27).

In Banat lies the Jungian notion of the "collective unconscious" and the seat of the human being's animal nature at its deepest level. The monstrosity of Banat's actions is dictated by the instinctive archetypes of the primordial thoughts that belong back in some primeval stage of human evolution and semiconsciousness. Jung states in many places that the presence of universal archetypes in dreams proves the existence of the unconscious.[8] Accordingly, Ambler gives Graham a dream worthy of archetypal analysis, when Graham reflects on his descent into the primeval swamp in an effort to preserve his own life: "He was a man alone, transported into a strange land with death for its frontiers. . . . His mind wandered away into an uneasy doze. Then he dreamed that he was falling down a precipice and awoke with a start" (141). Graham has slipped just as easily into the world of the savage and the brutal; his fall into the underworld of the unconscious reveals his own brutishness when he suddenly finds himself a man who will do anything to get his hands on a gun. The shadow is but another self. Graham risks the loss of his prized, virtuous, conscious self. The chasm into which he falls is the cleft of the modern psyche.

The other mask of evil is embodied in Haller—it is the mask of civilization that has surrendered to the facade of culture superimposed over the will to power. Ambler creates a graphic illustration of the twin masks in a diptych-like portrait of Banat and Haller. At the same dinner table at which Graham imagines the impossible insanity conviction of Banat, immediately following the characterization of Banat as the "subconscious mind running naked," Haller gives another of his little speeches. This lesson is about the Indo-European legacy of empire and greatness that has now fallen to the German people. Haller moves through history with giant strides: "From the Parthenon he wandered to pre-Hellenic remains, the Aryan hero tales, and the Vedic religion. Graham ate mechanically, listened, and watched Banat" (127). In this brilliant ironic episode, Ambler presents the two evil masks of Nazi Germany. The intellectual history of German romantic nationalism, based on the brooding philosophies of Johann von Herder, Goethe, and Nietzsche, is a form of national hubris—the collective consciousness of a culture that accepts the legacy of the will (and the right) to power. Together, Banat and Haller present to Graham a startling and harrowing glimpse of the modern mind and its ineluctable course in Nazi Germany. The latter, a political and ideological monstrosity, concretized the cleft between humanity's conscious and instinctual natures. In the modern world the inevitable lag of psychic evolution could not keep abreast of intellectual and scientific developments; the unconscious is left behind to seek its own self-preservation. With an engineer's knowledge of weird multipliers and an amateur psychologist's intuition of the reality of the Jungian dialectic, Ambler mapped out the horrifying world of the late 1930s.

Taken together, *A Coffin for Dimitrios* and *Journey into Fear* are Ambler's remarkably trenchant and prescient analysis of the events in Europe from 1935 to 1945. In many ways, Ambler novels are the fictional cognates to the Jungian essays that cover the Wiemar Republic and the rise of Hitler, going back to 1918. In a narrower perspective, Nazi Germany is the Jungian shadow that lurks at the edges of all six of Ambler's pre–World War II novels; it is the nexus of all of Ambler's studied readings of the interwoven threads of Nietzsche, Jung, and Spengler. Of these three major influences on Ambler, only Jung was alive for the outbreak of World War II (Spengler had died in 1936 of a heart attack, not long after an audience with Hitler). Between 1936 and 1947, Jung wrote a number of essays that deal with the German catastrophe and its implications for the study of the modern mind.[9] Amazingly, much of Jung's formal analysis parallels Ambler's fictional ironic and psychologically sharp etchings of a world rushing to its own destruction.

But the arrayed forces of darkness are held back and, temporarily at least, defeated in the novels of Eric Ambler. His fumbling, nonprofessional "heroes" survive through some chance occurrence or providential event. Latimer lives because of "a criminal's odd taste in interior decoration" (*Dimitrios,* 1), and Graham survives because of his final reliance on instinct and violence. Through it all, the quiet cognitive processes of deduction and reason singularly fail.

All this adds up to the raison d'être of the spy novel as shaped by Eric Ambler. The major premise of Ambler's argument resides in the dangerously thin veneer of protection that modern civilization offers the individual. The ages of Medieval faith and Renaissance decorum are past: Darwin, Freud, Frazer, and Spengler have triumphed. The world of the detective—the interlocking, visible puzzle pieces of Newton, Dupin, and Holmes—is inadequate in the face of technological warfare controlled by Dionysiac rage. The detective writer and the ballistics engineer had to doff the velvet of the human species and temporarily assume the characteristics of Dimitrios and other villains to survive. There is a little bit of Dimitrios in everyone. Violence and betrayal in the global village—this is the legacy of Dimitrios and an opportunity for the spy to pick up the pieces of the shattered Victorian world of rationalism. Or, in the words of Dryden, from the epilogue to *Cause for Alarm,* "Such subtle covenants shall be made, Till peace itself is war in masquerade." Ambler's persistent irony asserts that history itself is a concatenation of such masquerades.

Chapter Five

Picking Up the Pieces: From the Phony War to the Cold War

A Coffin for Dimitrios and *Journey into Fear* were published between September 1939 and July 1940, that period chronicled as the "phony war." *A Coffin for Dimitrios* appeared in the same month that Hitler invaded Poland, and it "had the distinction of being made *Daily Mail* Book-of-the-Month during the week that Britain, Germany and France declared war" (*Here Lies,* 154). *Journey into Fear* also made an uncannily well-timed entrance, and "was the *Evening Standard* Book-of-the-Month for July 1940, the month in which the Third French Republic ceased to exist and the Battle of Britain began" (*Here Lies,* 158).

Between 1940 and 1951, Eric Ambler, the meteoric prewar writer of mystery fiction, seemingly "ceased to exist." He served on active military duty during the war and then worked as a screenwriter with the Rank Organization, a British film company with Hollywood connections. Except for an aborted collaboration with Charles Rodda, an Australian popular writer residing in England, Ambler's daily habit of sustained writing had also "ceased to exist." After two painstaking revisions of the collaborative composition with Rodda (whose pen name was Gavin Holt; Ambler used the pseudonym Eliot Reed), Ambler resolved to pursue his own novel-length fiction. The effects of World War II took a long time to filter into Ambler's literary consciousness. Ironically, Ambler never did write a war novel. When, in the late 1940s and early 1950s he finally did return to writing lengthy fiction, the old routine did not come back easily. In *Here Lies,* Ambler addresses his self-imposed rehabilitation as a writer: "I had not written a book for ten years and in the army had lost the habit of a concentrated and solitary writing routine. The process of its recovery was slow. Besides, during those ten years the internal world which had so readily produced the early books had been extensively modified and had to be re-explored" (226).

The imaginary landscape to which Ambler returned, in a reprise of an Ixania summoned back some fifteen years after *The Dark Frontier,* was the Balkan country of his early novel. In *Here Lies,* Ambler leaves little doubt as to the events in Bulgaria that inspired his first postwar mystery; they were the "show trials" ordered by Stalin to be staged in that country (229). In a Western world that had to confront not only the wreckage of the war but also the trauma of Holocaustal war crimes, only the force of the law and the courtroom held out hope against lurking anarchy. The courtroom is the venue of civilization's reconstruction in the novels and the films of Europe and America in the 1950s.[1] It is the scene of rescue for that "internal world" ravaged by technological warfare and the genocidal thirst of modern dictators. The court of law, along with its various judgments, is the center of Ambler's next novel. It was based on a real case—one of those "show trials" of political prisoners in Bulgaria.

Judgment on Deltchev

In the aftermath of World War II, Eric Ambler faced an "internal world" thrown into the turmoil of conflicting ideologies spilling over from a Europe fractured by contesting political and economic forces. Ambler decided to make his literary comeback in the form of a foray into this welter of ideologies. *Judgment on Deltchev* reveals the many-headed monster of totalitarianism, the awful survivor of the slaying of the "blond beast" of fascism.

In a return to Ixania in *Judgment on Deltchev,* Ambler retains the narrative device of a visiting journalist. Here, however, the technological terror is not a nuclear bomb but modern propaganda. The journalist is actually a well-known British playwright who is asked by an American newspaper publisher to cover the trial in the Balkan state. (Following World War II, certain provisional government leaders were tried for betrayal of socialist principles.) In this manner, Ambler is able to retain the double consciousness of the split narrative of *The Dark Frontier* and at the same time develop an amplified theme and technique of a journalistic voice counterpoised to the heavy hand of state propaganda. In this latter regard, the country revisited in *Judgment on Deltchev* retains the spiritual landscape of the earlier Ambler with the accretion of an Orwellian atmosphere. What Orwell had done in *Down and Out in Paris and London* (1933) was to share with Ambler a politically charged odyssey into the shadowy world of colonial countries and hint at a catastrophic end to European hegemony. Orwell's vignettes of the early 1930s smack of the Ambler characters' sense of impending danger and demise. Like Ambler, Orwell had independently developed the curious perspective that both celebrated and feared the return of the Dionysiac and the demise of Western European rule; both British writers echoed the Spengler doctrines, without the reverberations of German romantic nationalism.[2]

By the time Orwell and Ambler came to write after World War II, they continued to agree that one of the principal instruments whereby imperial powers still controlled other states was in the corruption of language. And the continued need to corrupt language was even more paramount in order for the imperialists to deceive themselves in the wielding of an awful power. Orwell's 1946 essay "Politics and the English Language" could almost be a primer for the language and the criticism of the predicament of Ambler's focal character, Yordan Deltchev, as he confronts his torment in his conflicted assumption of total state power. The need for self-deception in an autocratic and totalitarian government is the moral dilemma of Yordan Deltchev, the once mighty leader and now disgraced defendant in a trial of international importance in Ambler's Orwellian Ixania. The many judgments in *Judgment on Deltchev* entail much more complexity than the legal wranglings at the trial's Orwellian charade.

The opening chapter of the novel is partly an extended rumination on the Orwellian theme of the disillusioning betrayal of socialist ideals by party leaders, partly an overview of postwar internal struggles for power within the Balkan states, and finally a blending of the fictional Deltchev story into the first two elements. Peter Lewis, in *Eric Ambler,* is absolutely correct in stating that the imaginary trial of Deltchev is representative of what happened in most Eastern European countries liberated by the Soviet army after the occupation of Nazi forces during the war.[3] Anticipations of Le Carré are heard in Ambler's depiction of the historical background as the forces of the cold war gather greedily amidst the wreck of ideologies and ideals.

The ideological jungle into which Foster, the British playwright-as-journalist, steps is both dangerous and violent. Foster is prepared for a travesty of justice and is preeminently qualified to portray the proceedings as part Stalinist ritual and mostly excessive theater. He is not disappointed; but he is not prepared for the complexity of the truth, especially when it masquerades as part of the falsehood of propaganda's political theater.

After four days on a train, Foster is met in the capital's Central Station by his employer's local representative, Georghi Pashik, a short, unpleasantly odoriferous, flabby man in rimless glasses and a worn-out (and unwashed) seersucker suit. In an outer pocket of the suit is arranged an array of fountain pens from Passaic, New Jersey. Foster astutely picks up on the pens as, in fact, a clue to the real character of Pashik; he rapidly composes his observations: "I think it was the fountain pens that identified him for me. He wore them like a badge."[4] This drab personage belies, as Foster says momentarily, "a man of destiny" who will escort the foreign journalist into the dark, many-roomed mansion of Balkan internal politics.

Pashik's immediate cautionary advice to Foster aggravates him. Pashik subtly but unmistakably informs Foster that all of his dispatches are subject to state (Propaganda Ministry) censorship. Pashik sounds very much the pawn of the state when he tells Foster that he, as a guest of the country, should not "prejudge the trial by sending hostile matter" (13). Pashik further insults Foster by telling him to enjoy the expense account supported by Western capitalism and perhaps even acquire an idea for a new play about life behind the Iron Curtain. Then a telling exchange occurs. Foster asks Pashik whether he is a member of the People's Party; Pashik good-naturedly dodges the question, but does answer another question, unconsciously, in a more pronounced American accent. He turns out to be a pro-Western Americanophile. It is one of Ambler's masterful strokes of irony and prophecy.

Pashik helps Foster pick up his trial permit from the Ministry of Propaganda and then delivers him to his hotel. The trial is to begin the next day. As Pashik leaves Foster for the evening, he hands him the news agency's file on Yordan Deltchev, the former head of the provisional government now accused of plotting to assassinate the head of the current regime, the People's Party Government.

Foster spends much of the night reading through the file carefully. What he discovers is a baroque history of internal politics and power struggles going back to the mid-1920s. Beginning in that period between the wars, Yordan Deltchev had risen steadily through the ranks of the Agrarian Socialist Party. Twenty years later, Deltchev had been instrumental in forecasting the failure of the German Nazi army in the Balkans, and he headed the Committee of National Unity and then the provisional government under that banner. The reference in the name to "unity," however, became a misnomer as the two principal factions (both socialist) polarized along the old prewar party lines after the general collapse of the Third Reich. It became politics as usual in the Balkan state, as the old parties jockeyed for position and aligned themselves with either the Russian or the Anglo-American hegemonies. Yordan Deltchev and the Agrarian Socialists held the upper hand, until Deltchev made the fatal miscalculation of calling for free elections. The opposition, led by Petra Vukashin, initiated a campaign against Deltchev, allegedly revealing his pro-Western sympathies and a secret stash of loot deposited abroad. Finally, Vukashin had Deltchev arrested, with solid evidence that Deltchev had conspired to assassinate the opposition leader. Curiously enough, Deltchev would have been the government leader had he not impulsively called for the elections during an otherwise planned radio speech. Deltchev now stood on trial in a country in which he might have held sway.

As the trial begins the next day, Foster describes the courtroom setting as "curiously reminiscent of a royal visit to the opera" (29). With that reference, Foster introduces a long skein of analogies between the trial and the stage—it is an exercise in political theater. At the end of the trial's first day, Foster unequivocally says: "I felt as if I had been to the first night of what had seemed to me a very bad play only to find that everyone else had enjoyed it immensely" (32). Having expressed such sentiments to Pashik, the latter responds: "Still, I expect that you'll make a play out of it sometime, won't you?" Foster then learns that daily summaries of the trial have been prepared for the press by the Ministry of Propaganda, and in fact these bulletins are the only version Foster can use in his dispatches to the foreign press. Foster objects vehemently to Pashik's collusion with the state authorities, to which Pashik retorts with a philosophical precaution.

Pashik's warning may sound familiar to Ambler readers; it is the warning of Colonel Haki to Latimer that academic murder is no preparation for the dark underworld of treachery and violence—art is no match for the realities of life. The superficial complexities of appearances in a fictional work of murder or politics are mere pretexts to the mysterious and inexplicable realities that swirl around power and greed. Pashik's warning to Foster comes straight from the Colonel Haki school for would-be detectives: "You are a stranger here, Mr. Foster. You look on our life from the outside. You are interested in the trial of a man whose name you scarcely know because his situation seems to you to contain the elements of a spiritual conflict. Naturally so. You are a writer of fiction and you make the world in your own image. But be careful. Do not walk upon the stage yourself. You may find that the actors are not what they have seemed" (34).

Like his forerunner, Latimer, in *A Coffin for Dimitrios,* Foster finds that every path in this maze of Balkan intrigue leads to center stage. And the actors are never quite what they seem, even in simple matters such as innocence and guilt. In the ambiguous words of Petlarov, Deltchev's former legal clerk and secretary, when he too advises caution before judgment on the part of Foster: "The lie stands most securely on a pinpoint of truth" (43). Foster begins to realize that he is getting dangerously close to stepping onto a stage of ambiguous shadows.

On the second day of the trial, the first witness for the prosecution is none other than the head of state, Vukashin. Minister Vukashin is a "small-part actor" who is a successful politician; unfortunately for him, he is not a skillful polemicist in the debate that is allowed to erupt between him and the defendant. The prosecution's fabricated charges unravel a bit with Vukashin's cross-examination by Deltchev. Vukashin is unable to answer Deltchev's claim that the contact with the Anglo-Americans was approved by the whole National Unity Committee. Having taken the high forensic ground, Deltchev then shocks the courtroom by revealing that the state has withheld his insulin injections for diabetes for the past five weeks (an actual event in a Bulgarian show trial according to Ambler in *Here Lies*).

The prisoner's remarks are then struck from the court record and the case is adjourned. Foster sits in silence, while Pashik tells him that he has just heard a great man speak. Foster's mind wanders to a long quote from the Platonic dialogue, *Crito,* in which the integrity of Socrates humiliates the posturing judges of ancient Greece. Foster then recognizes the scale of the political theater that has been enacted before him: "This, I thought suddenly, was more than just the crooked trial of a politician by his more powerful opponents. Here, epitomized, was the eternal conflict between the dignity of mankind and the brutish stupidity of the swamp" (55).

From this point onward in the novel, Ambler hits his stride as a prose stylist. The twisted convolutions (it is a complex plot) of political intrigue are matched by Ambler's intricate and subtle sentence structures. Gone are the stereotypical cartoon characters and the sometime wooden dialogue of the earliest novels; Ambler creates character through a progressive denouement of that character's increasingly complex inner world. *Judgment on Deltchev* delivers a tour de force for nearly every major character. These tropes are essential plays on the title word "judgment," for Ambler extends the meaning of the term far beyond the legalistic within the courtroom. Ambler's highly developed manipulation of character and theme are interwoven within a leitmotif of appearance versus reality. Not one of the characters is as he or she appears.

Ambler also develops another of his hallmark techniques—the narrative device of "leap and linger." He combines two very different narrative styles, sometimes dwelling on a single event, such as the meeting with the surprising and mysterious Madame Deltchev, and then letting the narrative jump ahead of itself with an extraordinary revelation or ironic twist. For all practical purposes, Deltchev disappears from the novel after the second day of the trial; both Foster and the reader formulate their judgments on the disgraced Deltchev on the basis of third-party dialogue and narrative (a technique Ambler bequeathed to the consummate craftsman, Le Carré).

Throughout the novel, the word "judgment" is employed in various contexts. There is of course the formal pronouncement of the trial—a foregone conclusion—which will be the verdict on Deltchev. But, as Foster comes to discover, when he passes through three doors—the essential Ambler rite of passage—that lead to the central epiphanies of the novel, the judgment on Deltchev is linked with several other judgments. Besides the lesson of appearance versus reality, Foster learns a great deal about the web of human relationships. And that web vibrates to the elementary resonance of love.

The first door that opens to Foster is that of the home of the Deltchev family. Madame Deltchev is hardly what Foster had expected. After meeting Deltchev's daughter, Katerina, Foster is struck by the youthful and erect figure of a fashionably dressed Madame Deltchev. She grants Foster a guarded interview; but it is not until the last chapter that she discloses information about her husband that reveals the family secrets that are also state secrets. Madame Deltchev delivers the most incisive and condemning judgment on Deltchev when she informs Foster that Yordan did not have the stomach for power. Yordan Deltchev, according to his wife, tortured himself with deep and corrosive doubts about the nature of power. Her last words to Foster are: "Yordan always invites criticism" (227). As Foster hastens to exit and catch a train to Athens, he thinks again of the Platonic account of the "show trial" of Socrates. Foster reflects on the final judgment on Deltchev—it was Deltchev's judgment of himself; it is the doubt of the decent human being who questions the sovereignty and control that can be wielded by any other individual or government. The final—and original—judgment on Deltchev is that of his own conscience.

The second door of intrigue that opens to Foster is the standard Ambler portal to danger and death—the discovery of an hours-old corpse that enmeshes the protagonist in even more complicated entanglements. This door also introduces Foster to the dark underworld of the country's Officer Corps Brotherhood, an illegal syndicate with roots in the internal politics of the state. This organization corresponds to the Bulgarian (and other Balkan states') Internal Macedonian Revolutionary Organization (IMRO), which has played a leading role in the national movement in Macedonia since the 1890s. Ambler called this same group the fictitious Society of the Red Gauntlet in *The Dark Frontier.* Like a person lost in a haunted house, Foster comes to apprehend the reality of interconnecting doors and mysterious passages. The Officer Corps Brotherhood, once nearly extinguished by the conscientious Deltchev, is alleged at the trial to be Deltchev's instrument of assassination against the state. Foster is puzzled by Deltchev's laconic acquiescence to this charge. Madame Deltchev's final conversation with Foster dispels all of the mysteries surrounding the Brotherhood as the nexus of the network of relationships, and she further explains Deltchev's withering and heroic self-judgment.

The last door to open to Foster is the door to Pashik's apartment. Crossing this threshold brings Foster and the reader to the strangest turn of events of the novel; for Ambler, it is one of his supreme achievements as a mystery writer. The revelation within Pashik's empty apartment comes in the form of the walls. The sitting room is like that of other European living quarters except for the decoration of the walls, which are covered and dominated by "studies" of film stars (all women) and other American graphic art illustrations. Pashik is the secret sharer in the covert political philosophy of Democratic capitalism. The locked chamber reflects the closed chambers of a heart hidden but full of hope and humanism. Foster comments on Pashik's astonishing display of American popular culture:

> The startling thing was that for every Ann Sheridan, for every sandal-tying beach beauty, for every long-legged hour, there was a precisely arranged frame of advertisement pages. The nearest Betty Grable was surrounded by Buick, Frigidaire, Lux, and American Airlines, all in color. A sun-tanned blonde glistening with sea water had Coca-Cola, U.S. Steel, Dictaphone, and Lord Calvert whisky. A gauze-veiled brunette with a man's bedroom slipper in her hand and a speculative eye was framed by Bell Telephones, Metropolitan Life Insurance, General Electric, and Jello. The baffling thing was that the selection and grouping of advertisements seemed quite unrelated to the pictures. There was no wit, no hint of social criticism, in the arrangements. Many of the advertisements were not particularly distinguished as such. It was fantastic. (172)

Foster unwittingly uncovers Pashik's profound sympathies as an Americanophile. This new knowledge further uncovers a series of connections between Georghi Pashik and Yordan Deltchev, which both explain and confound many of Foster's assumptions about both men. Ambler seems to be playing with a bit of Bulgarian history here; the names of the two colonels who directed the 1934 coup that abolished political parties were Damian Velchev and Kimon Georgiev.[5]

The revelation of Pashik's secret beliefs and the deep source of his true political ideals is perhaps the major surprise of the novel. But does Pashik's pastiche explain all? Possibly not. The Ambler reader must remember the old ad agency copywriter who first found his professional literary eye and voice. Perhaps Foster cannot find symmetry in Pashik's arrangement of youth and the products of capitalism because the symmetry lies between Pashik's walls and the walls of the Ministry of Propaganda. Ambler's deep irony consists in the juxtaposition of two different kinds of propaganda—but propaganda nevertheless. *Jugen und Kapital* had, after all, produced under the pretext of destiny the worst forms of human behavior seen in modern history. Ambler's creation here indicts the foolhardiness of all political ideals and locates in them power's arrogance and the source of Deltchev's self-judgment.

Where is the saving grace in the barren landscape of self-delusion? The answer is in Ambler's final images of walls and a darkened theater. Each of the novel's central characters lives in a delusional world circumscribed by physical walls. When Foster first visits the Deltchev house on the outskirts of the Presidential Park, he is struck by the wall around the house. Madame Deltchev explains the wall to Foster: "[I]n all the countries of Europe that have lived under Turkish rule it is the same. To put a wall around your house then was not only to put up a barrier against the casual violence of foreign soldiers, it was in a way to deny their existence. Then our people lived behind their walls in small worlds of illusion that did not include an Ottoman Empire" (69). Foster then asks Madame Deltchev a question that he recalls poignantly at the close of the novel when he leaves her and her country: "Isn't it dangerous to deny the street?" And it is her answer that he remembers later, when much of the baroque tale has unraveled: "For my children, yes. For me, no, for I shall not try to impose my private world upon the real" (70).

Her final judgment on her husband stems from her blaming him for hiding behind the walls of an illusory national life. She believes her husband abandoned both family and state responsibilities by denying the dangers of the street, the outside world. Deltchev had the chance to impose a private world upon the real, but that private world was conflicted by duty versus conscience. Madame Deltchev retreats back behind her walls and maintains a facade of stoic agreement with her doomed husband. If she had really had her way she would have fiercely opposed his too gentle naiveté.

Deltchev's wavering in the face of wielding absolute power allows the opposition party to succeed—but its success and continuation are predicated on its ability to construct its own reality. Deltchev understands the nature of that reality. Having once lived in a colonial state behind the confining walls of imperialism, he resists the temptation to trade the small walls of his home for the illusion of wider walls of sovereign power. The walls of the Ministry of Propaganda are the bastion of this state, and it too contains within those walls its own truth—but only the approved versions of that truth are permitted to transgress. Foster, who is temporarily allowed inside, nearly dies trying to get back outside. The prison of totalitarianism in the Ministry of Propaganda is a microcosm of the larger prison state created in an Orwellian nightmare of the corruption of absolute power.

When Foster surreptitiously gains entrance to Pashik's apartment, he gets a glimpse of the third and last set of walls in the totalitarian state. Pashik's walls finally set him free, but that freedom requires a heroic act of dying. He is killed because of his pro-Western sympathies. Thus, those fountain pens from Passaic were indeed a badge that became Pashik's blood red badge of courage.

Having penetrated all sets of walls, Foster finally gets home to England. There he sees the final acts of the Deltchev trial in the projection room of a London newsreel company. And then and there he comes to understand the conflated metaphors of walls and the theater. Within the sealed and darkened walls of the moviehouse, Foster watches the presiding judge deliver the sentence of death; Foster thinks of the words of Socrates: "But, sirs, it may be that the difficulty is not to flee from death, but from guilt" (229). The absurdity of the modern political movie is two-fold for Foster: the stage and its actors have changed little in two-and-a-half-thousand years; Deltchev had judged himself innocent long before the trial's outcome. As Socrates had shown a long time ago, innocence and goodness are as dangerous as guilt and evil. The reader should return to Ambler's quote from Nietzsche's *Thus Spake Zarathustra* in the novel's prologue: "Many things in your good people cause me disgust, and, verily, not their evil. I would that they had a madness by which they succumbed, like this pale criminal!" Madame Deltchev would have agreed with Zarathustra; Yordan Deltchev should not have troubled to fight with his own Dionysiac devils.

The Schirmer Inheritance

Published two years after *Judgment on Deltchev, The Schirmer Inheritance* continues to explore the aftermath of World War II and likewise deals with political and ideological intrigue in the Balkans. Like its predecessor, *The Schirmer Inheritance* deals with the convoluted theme of the collapse of idealism after the betrayal by political leaders of collective aspirations. More than a decade before Le Carré put the polish on the gentle character of the quiescent spy-hunter Smiley, Ambler created the splendid and powerful drama of the last illusion after all other beliefs and ideologies fail: the need for love and family. In his eighth novel, Eric Ambler forged the alloys of political disillusionment and the Jungian process of individuation to construct the central themes and forms that would dominate for the genre for the next forty years. In Ambler's distinct footsteps after this complex and sophisticated 1953 novel come the variations on these themes in the work of Le Carré, Deighton, Burgess, and even Graham Greene. The spies, or the clandestine agents of some cause, who desperately desire the "attainable felicities of wife and hearth," to borrow Herman Melville's phrase, in their coming in from the cold of ideology and betrayal, may find an eloquent forerunner in this Ambler novel.

In *The Schirmer Inheritance,* a Philadelphia corporate lawyer is assigned an old case of intestacy and embarks on a journey to the Old World that reveals human motivations that overshadow self-preservation and greed. But before introducing the reader to the lawyer, George Carey, Ambler provides in a prologue a long account of a particular battle in the Napoléonic campaign in Prussia, begun in 1806.

In February 1807, at the town of Preussisch-Eylau, Napoléon met the combined but scattered forces of the Prussian and Russian armies in a bitter blizzard. It was one of the bloodiest of all of Napoléon's battles. Among the Prussian units participating in the action were the Dragoons of Ansbach. Having nearly won the day against Napoléon's troops, the Dragoons began to retreat in disarray as the Russian army pulled back. A seasoned veteran, Sergeant Franz Schirmer, was seriously wounded by a deep saber laceration to his arm, and he knew that the situation for his men and himself was hopeless. The Dragoons were professional soldiers and cared little for causes such as nationalism or territoriality. Ambler explains their ambiguous allegiance to the Prussian cause: "The conception of nationality meant little to them. They were professional soldiers in the eighteenth-century meaning of the term. If they had marched and fought and suffered and died for two days and a night, it was neither for love of the Prussians nor from hatred of Napoléon; it was because they had been trained to do so, because they hoped for the spoils of victory, and because they feared the consequences of disobedience."[6]

While his tattered and frostbitten unit retreated to the north with the Prussian corps, Schirmer hatched a plan for his own survival and turned south. Scarcely able to stay in the saddle, he rode into Polish Prussia and approached a single farmhouse with smoke rising from the chimney. Sergeant Schirmer hailed the inhabitants, but only a solitary Polish woman came to the front entrance. The woman and her aged father had heat and shelter, but no food. Schirmer solved the food problem by shooting his horse. The frozen carcass furnished enough fresh meat for the duration of the winter and the sergeant's convalescence. Schirmer stayed at the Dutka farm for eight months, got strong enough to hunt, and married Maria Dutka. In November 1807, Franz and Maria set out for Westphalia. They had two sons, and for seven years the family prospered. Then, in 1815, Maria became ill and died; moreover, the Treaty of Paris decreed that the Schirmer residence in Westphalia would revert to Prussian control. Franz Schirmer stood the chance of being discovered as a deserter. He remarried and changed his name to Schneider. The former sergeant had ten children by his second wife and died in 1850, a respected and successful man. The change of name affected all of Franz Schirmer's children except one: the eldest son was seven years old and registered for Prussian conscription. Lest suspicion be aroused, Karl remained Karl Schirmer. This peculiarity descends, more than one hundred years later, on the head of George L. Carey.

Now a fledgling attorney in a prestigious Philadelphia firm, Carey comes from a prominent Delaware family "that looked like an illustration for an advertisement of an expensive make of car" (15). George graduated from Princeton just in time for World War II. After a four-and-one-half year stint as a bomber pilot in Europe, he attended Harvard Law School and graduated cum laude. Thus, when Carey joined the firm of Lavater, Powell, and Sistrom, one of the most important firms in the East, he had justifiably high expectations of dealing with landmark cases and important public figures. When he is assigned to the Schneider Johnson case, it comes as a disagreeable disappointment. It is a case of an intestate fortune, with missing heirs probably coming out of the woodwork. Moreover, the case was more than twelve years old. A $3 million estate originated in a soft-drink tycoon's death in the 1920s in Pennsylvania; because of Pennsylvania law, any proven blood relative could be entitled to a share in the estate. By 1939, even the Nazis in Germany were producing fake relatives (the search for bona fide blood relatives had led to Germany in 1938). Now, in 1950, the Commonwealth of Pennsylvania wanted to know whether any living heir could be found. George Carey inherited the case of eight thousand claimants—a legacy of complex and daunting dimensions.

The senior partner who assigns the case to Carey more or less lets him know that his is to be a perfunctory exercise. The basement vaults need cleaning, and the state is most likely the logical heir in an old and time-consuming investigation. Two tons of dead-weight documents lie in a basement vault. Carey "had no difficulty in finding the Schneider Johnson records. They were parcelled up in damp-proof wrappings and had a storage vault to themselves, which they filled from floor to ceiling" (21). Like Latimer's in *Dimitrios,* Carey's quest for the legacy of a dead man begins in a subterranean vault—a bureaucratic "house of death." As both come to discover, when dealing with Dionysian dissemblers, certificates of death are not worth the papers they are forged upon.

On the Monday morning of the fifth week of Carey's review of the files, pure chance brings the case to life. An avalanche of parcels cascades down on the custodian. Blood pours from a cut over his eye, but he hands to Carey a heavy deed box that had been hidden in the stacks. Stenciled on the box are the words "Schneider—Confidential." Within the deed box are photographs and memoirs of the Schneider family, dating back to the patriarch's account of his "heroic" part in the Battle of Preussisch-Eylau in 1807. At this juncture, Carey's investigation crosses the path of the legacy of Sergeant Schirmer.

Carey is dispatched to Germany by the senior partners to resume the search abandoned there at the outbreak of World War II. After hiring an interpreter, Maria Kolin, in Paris, Carey picks up the trail of the Schneider/Schirmer family through the old prewar parish vicar now assigned to a hospital in Stuttgart. Father Weichs narrates a riveting tale that in turn leads to other informants and their narratives. This referential system of third-party narratives hearkens back to Dimitrios and Deltchev in a technique that might properly be called the "absentee protagonist." The technique usually culminates in a crescendo with the absent party's powerful entrance into the novel; the device contributes to both the matter and form of suspense.

After Father Weichs comes Frau Gresser, who provides the final and vital missing link of information. She had personally known the last scion of the Schneider lineage: Franz Schirmer, a sergeant in the German Nazi *Fallschirmjager* (paratrooper; note the middle syllable is the surname of the Prussian) corps during World War II. One hundred and forty years after his great-great-great grandfather had disappeared in Poland, Sergeant Franz Schirmer was missing in action and presumed dead in Macedonia, during the Nazi retreat from Greece. His death—that of the last living heir of the Schirmer inheritance—was never confirmed by German or Greek authorities.

The trail of the Nazi paratrooper leads from Stuttgart to Bonn, the site of the German army records. From Bonn, Carey and Kolin travel to Cologne and Geneva. After nearly two weeks of investigation, they ascertain that the second Sergeant Schirmer had been born in 1917 and joined the Hitler *Jugend* at age eighteen. From the Hitler Youth movement, Franz Schirmer had entered the army and moved from the combat engineers to the airborne training unit, the *Fallschirmjager.* He saw action at Eben-Emael and Benghazi; he was wounded in the former battle, but fully recovered. In Italy, in 1943, while working as a parachutist instructor, he had fractured a hip. After months of unsuccessful rehabilitation and physical therapy, the young sergeant was declared unfit for combat duty. He was then posted to the occupation forces in Greece, in the Salonika area. While leading a convoy of German supply trucks, Sergeant Schirmer's lead vehicle hit a mine and was ambushed by a militant band of Macedonian nationalist guerrillas. The ambush killed nearly all, and the sergeant was missing and believed killed. The Macedonian freedom fighters, related to the IMRO of *Judgment on Deltchev,* were not usually in a position to shelter and feed prisoners for very long. That Schirmer was dead was a foregone conclusion to the German army.

For George Carey, however, the story has a familiar ring. He postulates that Schirmer may have unwittingly recapitulated his family history. He wires his superiors in Philadelphia, and thinks aloud to his bright and resourceful interpreter. What does a professional soldier do when the ragtag army he is running with has its tail between its legs and survival is dicey? Carey tells Kolin: "It's better to stay where he is for a while. He is a resourceful man, trained to live off the country. He can stay alive" (87). Kolin scoffs at the possibility, but the next informant, a Red Cross observer in Greece, attests to the presence of many Germans there after the war.

The senior partners in Philadelphia send Carey to Greece, where he picks up the trail in Salonika. Colonel Chrysantos (a latter-day version of Haki) is the senior Greek intelligence officer in the Salonika area and is the contact for Carey and Kolin. He arranges for Carey to interview a former guerrilla leader, now imprisoned in Salonika. In a scene that calls to mind Le Carré's later scene between Smiley and the incarcerated Karla, the Spartan prisoner refuses cigarettes from Carey and then brandishes a short sermon on the easing of Carey's conscience. Carey will later remember the example of the wretched prisoner who refuses to concede one iota. Besides, the prisoner Phengaros seems to communicate encouragement to Carey, although he can say nothing.

A final search of the hill towns near the scene of the 1944 ambush leads nowhere; Carey is on the brink of quitting when he passes through an Ambler door—the door to his hotel room, and also the door to Sergeant Franz Schirmer. Carey returns to his Salonika hotel room to find a gunman with a British accent, a British soldier of fortune, who asks whether Carey wishes to meet the former Nazi paratrooper. The last seventy-five pages of the novel introduce Carey and Kolin to the subterranean world of freedom fighters who have sloughed off the fatuous husk of causes and ideals. Carey, like Latimer, learns there can be life after the death of political naiveté. Franz Schirmer is the leader of a former revolutionary band of Greek and Macedonian *andartes* who have learned that bank robbing yields a better subsistence than the violent overthrow of a repressive government that merely springs back up. Schirmer is the Dionysian trickster living in the hills and groves of arcadian Greece and Macedon. With death being that good, the sergeant really has to think about a return to the land of the living, even if the inheritance is ostensibly so lucrative.

The Schirmer Inheritance is a tale of the development and maturing of both George Carey and the second Sergeant Franz Schirmer. For each the tortuous trail of the Schirmer family legacy leads to self-knowledge and an understanding of the deep connections to the past. Just as Carey is later found by the ex-Nazi paratrooper, in a typical Ambler reversal of hunter and hunted, the search for the Schirmer heir leads Carey to knowledge of his own family history and inheritance. All of this is a result of Ambler's adroit manipulation of his favorite Jungian themes: the descent to the underworld in the company of one's own shadow and the return of the Dionysian trickster.

Carey's descent to the underworld begins with his literal descent to the company vaults in the Philadelphia law offices. The Schirmer inheritance is buried in a family tomb, even complete with the family secret taken to the grave. But Carey penetrates the region of the dead and the vault yields its secret to him in the form of the recovered deed box. In the box, both the deeds and the dead are revealed to Carey. The box also leads to the dying Mr. Moreton, the former legal investigator who had gone to Nazi Germany in 1939. Moreton himself is approaching the region of the dead, and he initiates Carey into the mysteries of the deed (dead) box as he becomes the guide to the descent that will eventually take Carey to the ancient land of Charon and the river Styx.

More than the departed souls of the Schirmer family are in the "dead box," for Moreton reveals to Carey that the box had been sealed by him in 1944 when "my son was murdered by the S.S. after escaping from a prisoner-of-war camp in Germany. My wife wasn't too well at the time and the shock killed her" (45). Moreton could not justify any action, legal or not, that would send millions of dollars to Germany. Thus, he sealed the box with another family's dead sons and secrets. Carey has arrived in an Odyssean underworld, where he finds dead military heroes and grieving mothers. Like a magical fetish, the box holds past secrets and points the way to deeper mysteries.

Carey's guide, the interpreter Maria Kolin, has as principal credentials having worked as a translator at the Nuremberg trials. But her past also includes a journey into the Nazi house of carnage. As a Yugoslav, Kolin had lost her whole family to the S.S., and she fights her own devils with a nightly consumption of brandy that would floor most others. Kolin welcomes the opportunity to open up and explore her past, which turns out to be linked with the Schirmer inheritance. She is a capable, bright, and polyglot guide into the labyrinth of European history.

As was the case with ancient mythological heroes' descent into Hades in order to solve some puzzle in the daylight world, George Carey comes to realize that the Schirmer inheritance, and the search for its living heir, is only part of a larger quest. Far up in the hills of Macedonia, outside of Salonika, Carey begins to sense his own metamorphosis. Faced with a final dead end, just before he passes through the door of his room moments later, Carey experiences a new sensation. He had been enjoying himself in this mazelike puzzle:

> Yes, there it was. The talented, ambitious, pretentious Mr. Carey, with his smug, smiling family, his Brooks Brothers suits, and his Princeton and Harvard degrees, *liked* playing detectives, *liked* looking for non-existent German soldiers, *liked* having dealings with dreary people like Frau Gresser, disagreeable people like Colonel Chrysantos, and undesirables

> like Phengaros. And why? For the value of such experiences in a corporation law practice? Because he loved his fellow men and was curious about them? Rubbish. More likely that the elaborate defences of his youth, the pompous fantasies of big office chairs and panelled boardrooms, of hidden wealth and power behind the scenes, were beginning to crumble, and that the pimply adolescent was belatedly emerging into the light. Was it not possible that, in finding out something about a dead man, he had at last begun to find out something about himself? (124–25)

Carey's final descent into the last chamber of the underworld is shepherded by a gunman with a Cockney accent. Arthur, like Sergeant Franz Schirmer, is officially dead; but together they rule over a forgotten band of guerrillas who have flourished long after the politicians betrayed them. Facing death themselves, Carey and Kolin enter into this dead zone and find the sole living heir to the Schirmer inheritance. Because of his unwitting recapitulation of his family's story, Sergeant Franz Schirmer stretches the dead zone 140 years back into German and family history. The real legacy of the Schirmer inheritance is the genius for survival; in the land of the dead Carey discovers the legacy of the gift of life. In the bowels of this underworld no demonic figure reigns. Carey finds the modern incarnation of the trickster.

The encounter with the Dionysian trickster in the underworld recalls Jungian themes. Though Ambler's deployment of philosophical subtexts is far more subtle in his postwar fiction than in his prewar fiction, the intellectual underpinnings are certainly there. In Jungian depth psychology, the process of individuation is the common denominator between the descent to the underworld and the trickster-hero. George Carey's metamorphosis in Macedonia occurs as his psyche "bumps into the shadow" of the unconscious and meets his alter egos in the shadows of Kolin and Sergeant Schirmer. The Schirmer inheritance transports Carey into the underworld of the unconscious and its well-populated domain. For Carey, it is the Jungian journey within the multifaceted self and its "other."

In "The Process of Individuation," by M.-L. von Franz, one of the chapters in Jung's *Man and His Symbols,* von Franz describes the Jungian imagery of the descent to the underworld: "The maze of strange passages, chambers, and unlocked exits in the cellar recalls the old Egyptian representation of the underworld, which is a well-known symbol of the unconscious with its unknown possibilities. It also shows how one is 'open' to other influences in one's unconscious shadow side. . . . The cellar, one can say, is the basement of the dreamer's psyche" (175–76).

With Ambler fittingly beginning the novel's journey into the unconscious in the cellar of the Philadelphia law offices, how does he conclude it? What is the nature of the transformation and self-knowledge induced by the pursuit of the Schirmer inheritance? As Le Carré later succeeds in showing in his novels, the answer is always fairly simple. After the convolutions of political ideology and dangerous intrigue, the therapeutic and restorative element is usually found in a human emotion. Sometimes it is love, sometimes it is revenge; but for both George Carey and Sergeant Franz Schirmer it is the lesson of consanguinity—the value of the blood and its relations that bind the individual to a family. The connection of blood to the past is the Schirmer inheritance. At the novel's resolution, when confronted with the fact that he is the sole heir to a fortune in America, Franz Schirmer surprisingly tells Carey that he needs some time to think about it—he asks for twenty-four hours. Schirmer tells Carey and Kolin to return to his mountain hideout on the next night and impresses upon Carey the importance of bringing the family papers and photographs—the contents of the deed box. As events unfold, it becomes evident that Schirmer had already made his decision.

Plans for the following evening are wrecked when Kolin is caught by Schirmer's men in an abortive attempt to bring in the Greek authorities. Part of her miscalculation lies in the fact that the hideout is in Yugoslav territory, across the invisible frontier. Schirmer and his fellow tricksters dwell in mythical and untouchable Macedonia, beyond the reach of the princes who had betrayed them after the revolution.

Kolin is confronted with the evidence of her treachery and is physically struck by Schirmer and locked away in the maze of the secret hideaway. But Maria Kolin, herself a trickster and survivor, has come home to Yugoslav Macedonia. Hours later, while locked in an adjoining room, Carey hears her "shuddering cry of passion" while being visited by Schirmer. Another Franz Schirmer finds another Slavic Maria in enemy territory, and Carey realizes that the legacy of the Schirmer inheritance continues and leaps forward from the present moment. Carey never sees either Schirmer or Maria Kolin again, although he is detained and entertained by Arthur, the ex-British commando, for another two days and three nights.

During his ritual interment (most certainly the Greek authorities would have presumed death and burial for the outsiders at the hands of the guerrillas), George Carey has a great deal of time to contemplate the implications of his involvement with the search for the Schirmer heir. Before he is finally released by Arthur, Carey is told that all that

Schirmer wanted was his family's papers and photographs. Carey is later left a letter, written and translated by Maria Kolin, from Schirmer:

> I am sorry that you will have no more valuable a reward than my gratitude. Yet that I offer you sincerely, my friend. I would have been glad to receive so much money if it had been possible, but not more glad than I am now to possess the documents you brought me. The money I cannot think of with great emotion. It is a large sum, but I do not think it has to do with me. . . . the American State of Pennsylvania should have it. My true inheritance is the knowledge you have brought me of my blood and of myself. So much has changed and Eylau is long ago, but hand clasps hand across the years and we are one. A man's immortality is in his children. I hope I shall have many. Perhaps Maria will bear them. She says that she will wish to. (196–97)

The great irony of finding the heir to the Schirmer inheritance is that, despite the search's necessary focus on the past, the actual finding of the heir incurs the recovery of the future—and that restoration involves both Carey and Maria Kolin in addition to Schirmer himself. The affirmation of the connections of blood—Schirmer's symbolic orphanage is nullified in his valorization of family and family history—somehow assures the future of the larger social network. After the collapse of political ideology and violent social action, the adhesive that provides the coherence to the social and individual fabric is found in the microcosm of human emotions. Long after the grandiose historical movements of Napoléon, Prussia, and even the Third Reich, the smaller histories of family and its private, ironic generations are the principal ingredients of the continuation and the understanding of human life borne forward. The two orphans of European history, Franz Schirmer and Maria Kolin, are wedded in a union of fragmentary historical and familial pieces; after the evaporation of war, ideology, and macrohistory, home and hearth are found in the microhistory of love and its narrow circle of protection. The *Fallschirmjager,* "the hunter who falls from the sky with the protective umbrella," in the transliteration of the German for "paratrooper," finds the purpose of his "fortunate fall" in "the other" worth protecting. The human heart is the *Fallschirmjager* in the innermost workings of human history. This is the mystery revealed to George Carey.

The parallel structure of the novel is evident at this point. Just as Schirmer and Carey reverse positions, both as the hunter of the other and the "keeper" of Miss Kolin, their families are now juxtaposed in contrasting portraits. *The Schirmer Inheritance,* as constructed by Ambler, is in reality a tale of two families. From the opening pages of the novel, George Carey is presented as the scion of an important Delaware family of professional aristocrats; and it is he who will supposedly transport the history of the Schirmer family, with all of its weight of history, to the missing heir. But the hunter becomes the other. Part of Carey's journey of self-discovery is the shock of learning the truth and the power of the blood's network of relations. Simply stated, Carey discovers the distinction between family as social construction and the biological construction of bloodlines as identity. The oppositions are depicted in the photographic representations of the very different family histories: the old Schirmer family photos versus Ambler's curiously commercial and sterile portrait of the Carey family:

> George Carey came from a Delaware family that looked like an illustration for an advertisement of an expensive make of car. His father was a prosperous doctor with snow-white hair. His mother came from an old Philadelphia family and was an important member of the garden club. His brothers were tall, solid, and handsome. His sisters were slim, strong, and vivacious. The whole family, indeed, looked so happy, so secure, and so successful. . . . They were also exceedingly smug. (15)

The Carey family seems to belong in a fairy tale, while the Schirmers are participants in an epic adventure. The problem with the fairy-tale portrait lies in its sterile remove from the flux of life—it seems immutable. The Schirmer inheritance thrives, on the contrary, on a vitality that breathes the flux of historical event and flourishes on adversity. The difference between the two families is that one is the product of history and the other is the agent of historical change. George Carey undergoes a metamorphosis in Macedonia in which he changes from the former to the latter. The absence of vitality and the financial security of the Carey family represent a kind of death. In some ways, Carey's family is also in the deed (dead) box. Carey's sojourn in the underworld of the dead brings him to his shadow—the trickster who is also a clown—and he rises on the third day in Macedonia from the dead, laughing.

Jung called the process, the transfer of psychological hegemony within the individual from the conscious to unconscious factors, *enantiodromia,* a "running the other way." Jung borrowed the term from Heraclitus, the ancient Greek philosopher who taught that everything in time turns into its opposite.[7] The agency of the trickster, which is the real Schirmer inheritance, is the Hadian instrument of transformation and reversibility that produces a double *enantiodromia* at the novel's conclusion. Sergeant Franz Schirmer, renegade soldier of misfortune, runs the other way to consanguinity and family responsibilities; George Carey runs the other way as the dutiful son and lawyer who can laugh at the absurdities of financial legacies and legal justice. Having penetrated the region of the dead, he can only laugh at the joke of existence and its implicit absurdities.

In an illuminating essay, "The Trickster and the Sacred Clown, Revealing the Logic of the Un-speakable," Thomas Belmonte describes the Jungian processes of individuation and *enantiodromia* through the encounter with the negations of death and the trickster:

> The Greek trickster, Hermes, was the patron of herdsmen, thieves, graves and heralds. He was the god of boundaries and of those engaged in the risky business of crossing them. Like Charlie Chaplin's tramp, perpetually hopping from the wrong to the right side of the tracks (until claimed by infinity), the trickster-clown gives us a fleeting glimpse of the process of creation as order and chaos in alternation. In the clown's laboratory of far-from-equilibrium states, structure is renewable only if it is able to make contact with its negative.[8]

The Apollonian Carey confronts his Dionysian shadow in the shapes of the trickster and clown—Franz Schirmer and his sidekick, Arthur—far up in the hills of mythical Macedonia. Carey encounters a supposedly nonexistent band of Bible-quoting ("Put not thy trust in princes," quotes Arthur), bank-robbing pranksters in a land that supposedly does not exist. In this fantastic setting, Carey and Schirmer exchange their positions; they reverse polarity in several sets of opposites, to include freedom versus structure, orphanhood versus family belonging, communal versus individual identity. The resultant tableau is one of harmony and equilibrium.

The departure of the trickster allows for the liberation, both literal and figurative, of Carey from his underground hideaway. Arthur, the deadly clown, leaves abruptly also, and hints to Carey that Miss Kolin has left voluntarily with Schirmer, and she was "radiant as a bride." Carey asks of their whereabouts, but Arthur only hints at the region of Schirmer's legendary revolutionary actions—the Mount of Grammos. On a mountain in Macedon, not far from Olympus, the *hierogamos,* or sacred marriage, of trickster and anima signals a divine comedy of human players in which past and future, friend and foe, are wed in a marriage made in myth.

The last laugh in this comedy of human history goes to Carey himself. As George Carey emerges from the prison-tomb of his three-day incarceration, he walks back up into the daylight world laughing at the whole situation: "George wondered why it was, then, that he kept laughing to himself as he walked on towards the frontier" (197). Carey's is the laughter of the trickster-clown, laughter, as Belmonte describes it, "that degrades and materializes as it digs a bodily grave for a new birth" (Belmonte, 52). The frontier to which Carey hastens is the transformed state of restored psychic life. Having bumped into his shadow and experienced his self as deadly trickster and homicidal stranger, he has seen the enemy within.

Carey laughs at the human comedy of reversibility. The shadow of "the other" that hung over the West during those postwar years of the 1950s, however, adds another, more deadly dimension to the historical context of *The Schirmer Inheritance.* The fear of the other, and its shadowy, invisible presence that might destroy the safe and known world of the West was the paranoid fantasy of the cold war and McCarthy era. It was also the moment of return for the novel of espionage, suspicion, and betrayal. Eric Ambler had wanted to explore the shape and contours of the inner world as he returned to the art of his long fiction. In *The Schirmer Inheritance,* he provides a modern simulacrum of Dante's vision of hell; it depicts a world that fears Jungian reversibility as an inevitable betrayal. The cold war signified "the Devil" to be found in all "others":

> The real and present danger facing the postmodern mind was, for Jung, the breakdown in communications between the diverse regions of the psyche. Deprived of the oral-mythic system of maps and messengers, the self would, at best, come to experience itself (recalling Camus) as a disembodied, potentially homicidal, stranger. At worst, entire populations might suddenly find themselves in the grip of a terrifying psychedelia, dominated by an addictive and compulsive wish to kill an insurgent enemy—the "jew-nigger-commie-gook or flaming fairy" within. Whatever his own problematic relationship to the racist alternative was, the older Jung finally knew that the trickster would have the last laugh at Armageddon. (Belmonte, 52)

This is the last laugh of the novel, and Carey shares it with all the heirs of the Schirmer inheritance. Only princes and other fools indulge in the fatuous fantasy of exterminating the "other." The gift of laughter is the Schirmer inheritance.

Chapter Six

Facing East: The Orientation of Eric Ambler

In Euripides' drama *The Bacchae,* an Attic tragedy with distinct Asian hues, Dionysus is identified with his Asian origins and the Oriental mystique. Pentheus, king of Thebes, is destroyed by his mother and her sister Bacchantes; he is punished for refusing to recognize the power and the divinity of Dionysus. The play concludes with a choral recognition of the universal power of the Dionysiac cults and their resonance in human behavior and thought. In *The Birth of Tragedy,* some twenty-five centuries later, Nietzsche posited the same hypothesis vis à vis the waning of the Western European monarchic political system, which Nietzsche partially viewed as the eternal return of the irrepressible Dionysus. Nietzsche's canonical writings coincide with the German, French, and British monumental colonial enterprise in Asia and Africa.

Nietzsche's excursion into the genesis of Greek drama, at the time of intense and hegemonic European intervention in Asian cultures and politics, is prefigured in Euripides and Aeschylus by at least two themes. The first is the indelible line that is drawn forever after between two continents: Europe is hegemonic and the representer; Asia is the subaltern and the represented. Literary critic and cultural comparativist Edward Said wrote eloquently of this phenomenon in his 1978 book, *Orientalism.* "It is Europe that articulates the Orient," he says, "this articulation is the prerogative . . . of a genuine creator, whose life-giving power represents, animates, constitutes the otherwise silent and dangerous space beyond familiar boundaries."[1] The second theme of "Orientalism" is that last insinuation—the Orient is a dangerous and inscrutable place. The whole notion of Western rationality is undermined by the allure of the Dionysian mysteries that challenge the Greco-Roman basis for the "Western mind." And by extension, the sovereignty of "common sense"—that consensus of rationality—is threatened by other forces that may in turn topple the body politic. Thus, the state may be equally placed at risk by the Oriental dynamic (Said, 56–57).

This long encounter with the East—both Near and Far—is the taproot that gives depth and sustenance to the next brace of books by Eric Ambler. Ironically, as Ambler was preparing to move to California (the ultimate Golden West) in the late 1950s, he turned his intellectual gaze in the other direction, upon the source of his perennial themes of "the other" and "danger"; the underlying origins of his intellectual fascinations and literary imagination moved beyond the Balkans and riveted on the East. His next cluster of novels includes *State of Siege* (1956, published in England as *The Night-Comers*), *Passage of Arms* (1959), *The Light of Day* (1962), *Dirty Story* (1967), and *The Levanter* (1972). Two other novels—*A Kind of Anger* (1964) and *The Intercom Conspiracy* (1969)—were also written in this time frame and will be covered in the next chapter; the Oriental grouping represents a cohesive exploration in a new direction for Ambler. A more circumspect opinion might say that the direction and issues are similar to the early Ambler; but in his quest for the origins of historical and political issues in the Western mind, he comes full circle to the East and that murky median where East meets West—his old favorite, Istanbul.

In the very image and symbol of Istanbul—a city that is literally split by the line between East and West—Ambler confronts the complex mythography of Orientalism. His previous work has always taken the somewhat naive Western European (novelist or engineer or journalist) into the maze of the Orient and then exposed him to the labyrinthine Dionysian power (remember Latimer first glimpsing the death mask of Dimitrios in the Istanbul morgue). The same pattern persists for a while in this Oriental cluster, and then that lineage of protagonist gives way to a new kind of Ambler character—the double-heritaged hero who inherits the legacies of both East and West. In *The Light of Day,* and in that figurative literary dawn or birth of a new Ambler character, Arthur Abdel Simpson makes his debut (he returns in *Dirty Story*) as a character whose life is split in two as half-British and half-Egyptian and then endangered in a city split in two over the Bosphorus Strait, representing the long European encounter with Orientalism.

As with his anticipation of the atomic bomb, Ambler's skeptical view of decolonization and Orientalism anticipated that of later historical and postmodern pundits. Before Ambler focused in *The Light of Day* on the hemispherical and bicameral consciousness of Arthur Simpson and the Istanbul metaphor of the (literally) "Middle" East, he wrote two novels set in the Far East (Southeast Asia) outposts of Indonesia and Malaysia. Before centering on Istanbul's cleavage of geographical and geopolitical

Orientalism, Ambler must first explore the periphery. Both literally and figuratively, in the Ambler canon, all roads lead to the modern colossus of dual existence and identity—the West's ultimate confrontation with its Asian origins on the shores of the bicontinental Bosphorus. One of those roads begins in the Indonesian archipelago.

State of Siege

The Schirmer Inheritance leaves the regenerative hero, George Carey, with the gift of laughter as the turned-table Dionysian legacy from the trickster-guerrilla. In Ambler's next novel, *State of Siege,* the British engineer Steve Fraser is picked up in similar circumstances in an Indonesian island republic torn by postcolonial power struggles. Taking a page from Orwell, and perhaps even from the East Indies of Joseph Conrad, Ambler begins a five-novel exploration of the old theme of Western commercial exploitation (the former villainy of early novels in the machinations of the arms merchants Cator and Bliss) against the larger historical canvas of the aftermath of decolonization in Southeast Asia. The contemporary reader of *State of Siege* can retrospectively ask why, in fact, the architects of American policy on Vietnam did not read Eric Ambler in 1956.

As usual, Ambler's uncanny reading of imminent world events is striking in the novel's unsettling prediction of the emergence of the Asian quagmire and the absurd postimperial hegemony of the West. Through his perceptive reading of the East, Ambler himself begins to transcend his own restrictive Orientalism and to develop a remarkably non-Western, nonhegemonic perspective that will culminate in a cohesive and thematic epiphany in *The Light of Day.* Transcending Western consciousness is not the least of developments in these novels; the metamorphosis of Eric Ambler's curious "orientation" entails his coming to terms with the delimiting Orientalism of the Western intellectual. Between *State of Siege* and, two novels later, *The Light of Day,* Ambler's perspective, and that of his principal characters, shifts significantly away from a narrow ethnocentrism.

Like its predecessor, *The Schirmer Inheritance, State of Siege* unfolds after Ambler provides a lengthy preliminary history—this time of the fictional island republic of Sunda, located in the archipelago of the Indonesian Straits. The history of Sunda is narrated in the first person by Steve Fraser, as he sits on a provincial airstrip waiting for a plane. After working for three years in the northern provinces on an internationally subsidized power and irrigations project, Fraser is on his way home to London. Or thinks he is. While waiting for the weekly Dakota from the capital, Selempang, he assesses his past three years against the larger backdrop of the republic's colonial and now postcolonial history. "Now that I was leaving the place I could look at it with friendlier eyes," he muses.[2] This observation could serve as the theme of the tale, as Fraser betrays his own prejudices toward an East Asian culture refracted, to borrow a phrase from Conrad, "under Western eyes" (from Conrad's novel of that name).

Fraser describes a Sunda that was once part of the Dutch East Indies. After Japanese occupation during World War II, the Dutch returned only to find a Sundanese National Liberation Front with an armed demand for independence. In 1949 Sunda declared itself a republic. The provisional government found, with echoes of Ambler's *Judgment on Deltchev* and *The Schirmer Inheritance,* that the old Machiavellian adage was accurate: armies of liberation are easier to recruit than to disband. By the time the provisional government, under General Nasjah, was ready to submit a draft constitution to the General Assembly, an insurgent force of three thousand guerrillas was operating in the central highlands under an ex-colonel named Sanusi. In addition, a religious element played a role insofar as General Sanusi was now a devout Muslim who issued a series of calls for a holy war by the "true believers" against the infidels in the capital who had betrayed an Islamic state at the moment of its birth. Again Ambler is prophetic: to the reader of the 1990s, his descriptions of Islamic fundamentalism and the military morass of postcolonial Southeast Asia are right on target.

The bulk of the action in *State of Siege* comprises the double entanglement of Steve Fraser with a Eurasian prostitute, Rosalie Van der Linden, and their capture by Sanusi's rebel forces in the center of Selempang. To the familiar tale of the dilettante's deadly encounter with danger, Ambler uncharacteristically adds sexuality. In a bold departure from past practice, Ambler's protoganist spends what might be his last moments alive in a steamy mix of sex and violence; Eros and Thanatos finally appear together, almost à la Hollywood, in an Ambler novel. Ambler discovered for himself an age-old theme, going back at least to the temptations in *Sir Gawain and the Green Knight:* the Dionysian value of sex in the face of imminent death.

The sexuality in this novel is further complicated by what seems to be the development of the character of the Eurasian prostitute. Rosalie Linden is, in the pejorative opinion of her peers, an outcast "half-breed."

Her father was in the Dutch army and her mother was local Sundanese; Rosalie's very presence is a bitter reminder to the now independent Sundanese of colonial occupation. When Rosalie and Fraser are caught by circumstances in the middle of a coup d'état, the Islamic forces under Sanusi show little regard for either of these colonial representatives. In the eyes of the Islamic rebels, the sexual services provided by the Eurasian prostitute to the foreign engineer become vivid testimony to the political and religious corruption of the provisional government. Fraser contemplates the rebels' repugnance to her: "For these men, with their desperate pride of race and hatred of Europeans, she already stood for treachery; and the fact that she was there with me made the iniquity of her existence doubly obscene. To kill us both might seem like an act of purification" (62).

What saves Fraser is a combination of his engineering skill and Rosalie's bicultural acumen. Her mind is as agile as her body; she and Fraser develop a relationship far beyond the physical. During forty-eight hours of shared mind and body in the midst of extreme danger, Fraser's attitude toward the East begins to change. Rosalie's tortured "half-caste" identity is instrumental in effecting a humanizing influence on a "skilled technician" who never acknowledged the human factor in his immersion in the Orient.

Another surprise in the novel is the character of Major Suparto. Beginning inauspiciously as a graft-mongering government thug, Suparto graduates to a higher scale as he becomes a key in the thwarted revolution and also demonstrates a profound humanism in his part of the treatment of the trapped lovers by the lawless rebels. Ambler chooses Suparto as an Asian voice for the seemingly, at least to Westerners, irrational behavior of the Sundanese political principals. Suparto is a foil to the Islamic nationalist, Sanusi; and each represents a facet of the inscrutable house of power and mystery that is Asia.

General Sanusi broadcasts a speech during the coup that might be lifted from any Middle Eastern newspaper story in the 1990s. Long before the deposing of the Shah and his royal family in Iran in 1979, Ambler had articulated the power of Islamic fundamentalism in recoil from European colonization and religious tyranny in the words of Sanusi: "The guilty will be punished. The Unbelievers will be destroyed. Colonial influences will be eliminated. The Faithful will rally to the standard of Islam" (46).

Sanusi's radical politics and religion are offset by the agent provocateur, Suparto. The ambivalent Suparto tells Fraser before the end of the novel: "[W]e must choose between evils. The Nasjah government is corrupt and incompetent, and foreigners laugh at us for it. But you have heard Sanusi . . . what has he to offer as the leader of the nation? More mosques in Selempang? Excellent. But what else? Only the discipline of men like Roda, men hungry for power" (105). Suparto concludes by suggesting that the Sundanese must be left alone to find their way through the residual postcolonial detritus of a fragmented history.

The lesson impressed upon Fraser by the two authentic voices of Rosalie Van der Linden and Major Suparto leads the technician to a consciousness that transcends the limited vision of Western eyes that Edward Said has termed "Orientalism." As a typical European, Fraser had lived in Sunda for three years and labored under his own ethnocentrism. The central progression of the novel is the cultural education of Stephen Fraser as he moves along a spectrum of ethnorelativism that begins with his own centrist biases (matched in the native culture by the fundamentalist Sanusi). As Fraser begins to understand the bicultural ambiguities (and political chameleon shades) of Major Suparto, who tries to explain away the worst while perpetuating the best of both worlds, he ultimately, unexpectedly, bumps into the true meeting of East and West at the fundamental level of interracial sex and love. In Rosalie Van der Linden, Fraser encounters not only the symbol of the humiliating colonial past but also the clear direction for a harmonious future.

Fraser and Rosalie meet at the aptly named New Harmony Club in Selempang, and Ambler seems to be taking a bold step toward not only sexuality in his work but also significant treatment of miscegenation. This unexpected humanistic education transports the distanced and somewhat racist postcolonial to culturally sensitized consciousness. When the money he bestows upon the Dutch-Indonesian prostitute is finally given, it is as a gift in an act of love. The money does not pay for sex and affection but rather represents an attempt to make restitution for the long history of colonial exploitation that made such exchanges between Easterner and Westerner nearly impossible.

Like *The Schirmer Inheritance, State of Siege* concludes with the provision of an impossible gift. In the latter, the gift of the silver box set with an amethyst in the lid is more important than the money it contains. The amethyst is the star of the East. It is recalled in Sanusi's key speech in which he excerpts the Koran: the amethyst is "the star of piercing radiance. Truly every soul has a guardian over it" (141). The original British title—*The Night-Comers*—was also taken from this speech. The night-comer is the soul, and its piercing radiance is the breakthrough of love and humanism in the surrounding cloak of darkness. The silver box bedecked with a precious and brilliant gem represents love that will illuminate even the darkness of racism and colonial hatreds. Ambler has returned to the central theme of *Judgment on Deltchev,* when the long night of muddled political ideologies and facile betrayals has ended, and the radiant morning star of love and its simple devotions transform the night-comer/soul.

Passage of Arms

Like *State of Siege,* its predecessor, *Passage of Arms* unfolds a tortuous travelogue plot in the steamy cities and jungles of Malaysia and Indonesia. Along the way, in the novel's charting of the passage of a cache of weapons and its depiction of the entanglement of the arms of the human embrace, Ambler calls to mind the double entendre of another postwar novel, Hemingway's *A Farewell to Arms.* Ambler furthermore explores the central motif of his Oriental cluster of novels by probing the complex and subtle set of relationships within the postcolonial legacy of arms and men (*and women,* to improve upon Virgil). The larger events of history take their toll even in individual private lives.

In this second novel of the Oriental grouping, Ambler departs from the easily detected East-West distinctions that mar *State of Siege* with a vague but noticeable pro-Western bias, the set of attitudes Said termed "Orientalism." In his 1993 critique of Eric Ambler, Peter Wolfe accurately describes the tonality of *State of Siege:* "*Siege* exudes some of the nostalgia for Empire that led Ambler to build *Frontier,* in which Cator and Bliss stood for capitalist evil, around the archetype of the Victorian gentleman-adventurer."[3] Wolfe is correct in characterizing Steve Fraser, *Siege*'s English narrator, as representing the perpetuation of racist insinuation and consciousness in Fraser's muttering, "I have always sympathized with those legendary Empire-builders who changed for dinner in the jungle" (*State of Siege,* 53).

Passage of Arms veers sharply away from the theme of European colonial virtues versus Asian native defects. By dispensing with a central character who would have to reflect a given point of view, Ambler creates a multiplicity of perspective and character that allows for various shades and ambiguities to blur the implicit Western bias. Ambler's narrative, as Wolfe notes nicely, belongs to a literary tradition that might well include Chaucer's "The Pardoner's Tale," Poe's "Gold Bug," and Hammett's *Maltese Falcon.* Those narratives portray the valorization of some object of material worth, which is essentially corrupt, as the object (and its objective correlative value, always blurring into a murky metaphorical stratum) affects the lives and actions of many people. Ambler uses a decidedly colonial objective correlative; *Passage of Arms* follows the trail of evil and vitiation as a cache of weapons is depicted as the destructive legacy of decolonization. The arms become the nexus of many individuals, nations, causes, and ideologies, binding life and death, good and evil, human culture and nature in a kaleidoscopic turning of events. The "passage of arms" traverses a course of corruption that shapes the lives and actions of individual humans long after the Dutch, French, British, and Portuguese have deserted their colonial outposts. The legacy of violence is as profound and ingrained as the "original sin" of exploitation and its consequence of human suffering.

The inciting force in *Passage of Arms* is an ambush of a band of Malayan insurgents by a combined patrol of Malayan and British army commandos. Ambler's opening stylistic gambit links the ambush to later seemingly random and trivial events: the theft of tarpaulins at a nearly rubber plantation and the removal of the wheels of the plantation manager's children's scooter. The manager, Mr. Wright, is oblivious to the proximity of danger and violence; and, in fact, "Mrs. Wright, a woman of character, calmed the servants and ordered fresh toast and tea so that she and her husband could finish breakfast."[4] This doomed preciosity of the myopic colonials recalls the unreconstructed ethnocentrism of Steve Fraser. The breakfast in the jungle resumes, but what issues from this minor disturbance is a "passage of arms" that will extend far beyond the provincial rubber plantation and reflect a fundamental transformation of that whole part of the world.

Girija Krishnan, the Indian clerk and supervisor at the rubber plantation, decides later in the day of the ambush to play detective. He notes the absence of cooking equipment on the slain rebels. He correctly deduces that the rebels had been supported by the local villages and that their real mission was to serve as a supply column for an arms cache further south. After months of combing the logical places, Krishnan finds the jungle hideout of the now-abandoned cache. Thinking the unthinkable, Krishnan begins to hatch a plan to sell the arms to the Indonesian black market and to use the money to buy British buses for his own rural transport business. Krishnan's hope is to actualize his boyhood dreams, which originated with his parents and their Bengali subservience to the British Empire.

Krishnan's father, an Indian soldier in the British army, was killed in action at Alemein. Before his death, his father had been brought to London and given grand treatment. At age six, young Krishnan remembers his father's triumphant return to Bengali: "He returned to India laden with souvenirs and fired with ambition for his only son" (7). The battle at Alemein changed all of that, as the only son was placed in a military orphanage at Benares for three years. At the end of the war, Krishnan's mother arranges passage for him, along with his five sisters, to Singapore, where the fatherless children become indentured servants to the mother's brother. In an ironic twist, this passage too is one of arms—but not the loving arms of a protective brother and uncle. Ambler sustains this double entendre throughout the novel in the interlocking strands of both kinds of passages: his potent theme is the inextricable linking of love and violence in the interwoven arms of an exploitative past. This multipurpose pun forms the ironic perspective at the very base of many of the relationships in the novel; for instance, the British ex-Captain and Mrs. Lukey are later principals in the business of running arms, and their marriage is also an arms business arrangement.

Through ingenuity, demonstrated again later by finding and selling the Malayan weapons, Krishnan is able to deliver his family from the bondage of his uncle. All that he takes, when he moves on to the managerial job at the rubber plantation, is a British bus manufacturer's catalog that had been one of his father's souvenirs from England. Like the weapons shipment later intercepted, the fugitive pieces of Empire leave a lasting mark and an enduring legacy. Even after the collapse of colonial designs, the gardens and jungles of Asia are invaded and dominated by the machinery of the West's technological hegemony.

Krishnan, however, is only the first of several key characters in a novel that essentially constructs a fluent and mobile tale following the course of an arms movement and not the actions of a single protagonist. The arms cache itself becomes the common denominator in multifarious movements by new characters in a variety of locales. From provincial Malaya, the business deal moves out of Krishnan's hands, and he does not appear again until the end of the novel. The commerce surrounding the sale and shipment of the arms weaves in and out of legitimate business and into the shadow world of agents provocateurs who move between Singapore, Saigon, Manila, and Sumatra. Into this vortex of corruption and danger sail an affluent American engineer and his wife, Greg and Dorothy Nilsen, of Wilmington, Delaware. Lured by a taxi driver in Hong Kong, Nilsen is duped into phony ownership of the weapons. The network of illicit arms commerce is a far-flung series of relationships, most of which are based on the exchange of cash. The passage of arms simulates a legitimate economy with a whole culture constructed around it. That culture, Ambler seems to tell the reader, is not much different from so-called legitimate societies that demonstrate a noble ideology as a veneer over the same merchandising of misery, violence, and death.

The essential and sustained metaphor in this novel without a central character is the image of a city. Lubuanga is the provincial capital of Sumatra, where Mrs. Lukey and the American couple are brought by the Indonesian rebels for the final transaction. Lubuanga is a port city where the natural confluence of rivers and the unnatural confluence of oil pipelines converge in an order mechanically imposed on the organic design. The Western machine has made an incursion into the Eastern garden. But the city, in Ambler's figurative language, has retained feminine and organic qualities. In a strangely unexpected way, the symmetry of the network of waterways in the river delta is matched and harmonized by the tree-lined streets and public gardens designed like towns in the Dutch hinterland. Ambler adds that the "effect was bizarre." Instead of linden and sycamores, there is Asian flora in all of its tropical luxuriance. On an empty pedestal that once supported a statue of Queen Wilhelmina, a hibiscus "rioted." The final effect is framed by Ambler in a sustained feminine simile: "The center of Lubuanga was like a respectable Dutch matron seduced by the jungle and gone native" (136). In a reverberation of Conrad's *Heart of Darkness, Passage of Arms* suggests that, despite the mechanical intrusions of the colonial military-industrial complex, the Dionysian return had not only survived but had in a strange syncretism prevailed toward a fusion of opposites in the organic and pastoral principle. Nietzsche himself might approve of such "passages."

The Light of Day

Like its main character, *The Light of Day* was born of a curiously double identity. The original manuscript, along with all of its researched materials, burned in a catastrophic house fire when Eric Ambler was living in Bel Air, California. With great patience and fortitude, Ambler rewrote the entire novel. In many ways, *The Light of Day* is the cornerstone of Ambler's discovery and construction of his second great theme (after the prewar construction of Jungian depth psychology as the first motif) of Orientalism and the Asian sources of the Dionysian eternal return. Ambler's coup in the examination of Orientalism entails his coterminous usage of the decolonization theme. Long before the quincentenary celebration of Columbus's first voyage to America raised widespread consideration of the impact of his legacy on native peoples, Ambler was examining the effects of imperialism and colonization on the locales he knew best—just to the East of the Balkans, where one can find the dawn of Western civilization and the epistemological light of day. In the twilight of the Levantine dawn, Apollo drags forth the chariot of the gods from dark Orphic and Dionysian mysteries. Nietzsche's "twilight of the idols" issues from that same dark frontier. In the half light and half darkness of the novel's image and symbol, Arthur Abdel Simpson, Ambler's main character, issues forth from both Eastern and Western origins as the "mongrel" example of a Dionysian spirit that outlasts and outwits the postcolonial suppressor.

As the narrator of *The Light of Day,* Simpson renders the tale in retrospect. The advantage of this perspective—one that Le Carré later adopted—is the mingling of present-tense action with occasional retrospective opinions and postmortem analysis. As Le Carré again demonstrates after Ambler's lead, the putative spy (or accidental spy or spy hunter) has a deep interiority that reinforces the old adage that "seeing (or espying) is believing." The retrospective spy is the one who has ostensibly survived to tell the tale; but the tentative terms of psychic survival always transpire in the ambiguities of a murky moral landscape.

Simpson begins, even before the action of the novel, in an ambivalent zone of moral persuasion. The son of a British Army officer, a lieutenant-quartermaster who was killed in 1917 on the Turkish front, Simpson was born in Cairo of an Egyptian mother. Now living in Athens and a journalist by profession, Simpson pursues the occasional sideline (when the rent is due) of running a car-hire business from the Athens airport. He has few qualms about occasionally fleecing an unsuspecting tourist by either bribery or theft. Simpson's hired auto, unbeknownst to guileless tourists, can take both the high road and the low road. But the low road eventually leads to trouble for Simpson, when he takes on as a passenger the beguiling and dangerous Mr. Harper, who draws Simpson into a convoluted plot that goes well beyond both petit larceny and the Athens city limits.

Simpson attempts to rationalize his sometime thievery by revealing that he had never stolen from anyone who did not first want to be taken to the red light district. He proceeds to fill in the history of his proper and British upbringing—by implication his substitute for genuine breeding and high moral character. After the death of his father, Simpson was admitted to a British school in Cairo. With his education subsidized by the army's association for the Sons of Fallen Officers, Simpson at age nine was sent to England for schooling there. Transported to England on a troop ship carrying a sick bay full of V.D. cases, Simpson upon arrival was boarded with a sister of his father in southeast London. While Coram's Grammar School at Blackheath was not like Eton or Winchester, the curriculum was traditional and the discipline rigorous. Simpson got on with the classmates, but because he had been born in Egypt he was called "Wog." He finally endeared himself to his schoolmates and ran afoul of the headmaster by composing and publishing copies of bawdy verse.

In the end, Simpson's considered opinion of the whole point of English public school education is the inculcation of a steadfast desire to maintain the facade of appearances—to "make him look and sound like a gentleman."[5] Through a multitude of flashbacks throughout the novel, Simpson regales the audience with his sardonic view of how the English school system has made him and many others paragons of breeding and character. Simpson harbors a deep hatred for the intellectual and moral supremacy that was wielded against him throughout his school days in England. As the half-Oriental (or technically African) and former colonial, he nurtures the hatred of the former slave for the former master, mostly because of the enduring superiority of the English gentleman at home and abroad. Simpson has experienced the reality behind the superficial facade.

Thus, once Simpson learns he was mistaken to take Harper for an American and an easy dupe at the Athens airport, he simmers at the eventual enslavement of his services, and even perhaps his civil liberties and life, at the hands of this neocolonial Anglo-German. Harper catches Simpson in the act of stealing traveler's checks after Simpson thinks that Harper has been "kept" in the red light district, thus ensnaring Simpson in a complex scheme engineered by Harper and his Anglo-German associates. Harper dictates a "confession" and forces Simpson to write it and sign it; it becomes a kind of dirty business contract that retains Simpson's chauffeur services. Simpson is to leave almost immediately for the Turkish frontier to deliver a Lincoln Continental to Istanbul for Harper's friend, Miss Lipp. If Simpson fails to comply with the terms of the contract, Harper will use the confession written in Simpson's hand:

> I . . . stole American Express traveller's cheques to the value of three hundred dollars. . . . I have stolen, forged and cashed other cheques in that way. . . . But now I find that I cannot go through with it. Because of Mr. Harper's great kindness to me during his visit to Athens and his Christian charity, I feel that I cannot rob him. By taking this decision, I feel that I have come out of the darkness into the light of day. I know now that, as a sinner of the worst type, my only chance is to make restitution, to confess everything. . . . . Only in this way can I hope for salvation in the world to come. (25–26)

The "confession" is clearly cast in the language of a "conversion"—a religious conversion. At first this rhetoric might seem puzzling, but it reflects the religious condescension of the Christian colonial to an ignorant infidel and thief of Muslim background. "The light of day" phrase is a smug reflection of patronizing European colonialism and superiority. The confession reminds Simpson of schoolday caning by the headmaster, which was preceded by a formal "request to be punished." The empire had required humiliation of both body and spirit. For the duration of Simpson's entrapment in the Anglo-Germanic grip—which turns out to be for the purpose of a jewel heist at the National Palace—he is reduced to the abject level of a colonial servant broken in both muscle and will.

Like all occupied colonials, however, Simpson plans his liberation and revenge, fueled by the hatred for scandal and hypocrisy engendered by his rigorous training in the British public school system: "One of the most valuable things I learned at Coram's was how to hate; and it was the cane that taught me. I never forgot and never began to forgive a caning until I had somehow evened the score with the master who had given it to me" (30). Simpson equates the academic master with the imperial master of the British colonies; the connection is an assumed and ethnocentric superiority of a system of values—along with political and religious biases—that brought about the very human union that procreated Arthur Abdel Simpson's conflicted existence and bifurcated identities. Harper's extorted "confession" dredges up all of Simpson's former hatreds of a system of arrogance and hypocrisy.

After Harper delivers the Lincoln that Simpson is to drive overland through Salonika to Istanbul for the absentee Miss Lipp, Simpson searches the car for illicit goods in what he thinks may be a smuggling operation. He finds nothing, even when he puts the car high on a garage lift. He decides that the empty car is a logical piece of contraband traffic that will be used to smuggle the other way—from Turkey into Greece.

That assumption is quickly crushed at the Turkish frontier town of Edirne, when the border police find that the car's cavities are stuffed with automatic weapons and grenades. Simpson is arrested and taken into custody by the Turkish secret police. General Haki (formerly Colonel Haki in *Dimitrios*) makes a cameo appearance on the telephone and arranges for Simpson's becoming a Turkish operative and double agent and for his release. Another "duplicity" is added to Simpson's dual-heritaged life. This series of dualities is significant, as Simpson continues his mission and arrives in the city that both splits and joins the line between Europe and Asia. Like Simpson, Istanbul draws its dual legacies from both East and West.

As the principals in Harper's circle of gem thieves gather in a villa outside of town on the European side of the Bosphorus, Simpson is drawn into their confidence and attracted to the surprisingly young and lithe Miss Lipp. In a scene of deep irony, Simpson is trapped in Lipp's apartment when she and Harper unexpectedly return. Before he can escape through a bathroom window, in a scene that recalls the voyeurism of the schoolboy's pornographic verse at Coram's, Simpson overhears a noisy and robust act of sexual intercourse between Lipp and Harper. Simpson's outsider status is emphatically portrayed in this unexpected scene. The reader can appreciate the "mongrel" colonial's distanced and disenfranchised position as he witnesses the Anglo-Germanic copulation; just such a union bequeathed to Simpson his dubious genealogy. The conjugation of the colonial masters only serves to further alienate Simpson, who is both dispossessed and (from the white woman's point of view) desexed. The total spectrum of his identity—including his sexual potency—is eradicated by his relationship to the Europeans.

Simpson's loss of sexual identity and his search for his absent father (discussed at length by Peter Wolfe in *The Art of Eric Ambler*) are integrally connected in Simpson's lucid recollection of one of his father's military vignettes. While awaiting interrogation in a holding cell in Edirne, Simpson remembers his father's advice about soldiers who get off easily by telling a spicy, but somewhat invented, alibi. Simpson's father had labeled these tales "well-sirs." The most memorable of the "well-sirs" went like this:

> Well, sir, I was proceeding back . . . towards the barracks in good time for lights-out and in a soldierly manner. Then, sir, just as I was passing the shopping arcade by Ordnance Avenue, I heard a woman scream. . . . The sound was coming from one of the shops in the arcade, so I went to

> investigate. . . . Well, sir, what I found was one of these Wogs—beg pardon, sir, a native—molesting a white woman in a doorway. I could see she was a lady, sir. . . . She [had] been on her way home to her mother's house . . . when this native had attempted to—well, interfere with her. (48–49)

The father's narrative is structurally juxtaposed to the later scene in which Lipp wields her privileged intellectual and sexual superiority over the hapless Simpson against the backdrop of the arcade of the Seraglio. As Simpson describes the Seraglio: "So the Seraglio today is a vast rabbit-warren of reception rooms, private apartments, pavilions, mosques, libraries, gateways, armouries, barracks and so on, interspersed by a few open courtyards and gardens" (106). The background setting for the power of the Ottoman—and Eastern—Empire now appropriated by both the intellectual knowledge and sexual prowess of the white woman, Miss Lipp, signifies the total and comprehensive humiliation of the colonized Asian male at the hands of a colonial European woman. Simpson's fractured identity suffers the same loss of prestige, power, and status as all of the East, and other former colonies, under the West's arrogant and corrupt Orientalism. In these five novels constructed around Orientalism's ethnocentric perspectives, Ambler rendered literary treatments of this historical and political phenomenon as the world was coming to terms with a renewed international spirit of nationalism and independence. World War II had witnessed the rise of a new American empire. In the late 1950s and 1960s Ambler was still exploring themes and issues stemming from the decline of the European West. Spengler had pointed in the right directions. Ambler felt compelled to explore those Spenglerian directions in the aftermath of empire and diminished spheres of power; he signaled the rise of Third World peoples.

The main plot of *The Light of Day* is an exquisitely planned looting of the Turkish royal treasury, principally its legacy of jewels and gems (its natural resources commingled with a national history), by a British and German gang. Symbolically speaking, the looting of Asia by the old European powers is continued, right down to the involuntary enslavement of Simpson, progeny of the unequal union of West and East. In a final ironic note at the conclusion of the novel, the theme of imperial European reprise is completed when the thieves escape from the Istanbul airport on a flight to Rome—the Eternal City and the seat of the ancient Roman Empire, the first of the Western powers to colonize the East. In his development of this Orientalism theme, Ambler follows Rudyard

Kipling and George Orwell. Like them, he was sensitized to the inevitable cycles of history and political power; also, like his predecessors, he knew of the veneer of civilization, especially of its thinness and fragility when it was imposed from above. In the East, the veneer of Western civilization was neither civil nor ever totally discrete in its confrontation with Orientalism.

Ambler's treatment of these themes in his Oriental novels can be usefully explored and understood in the additional light of Said's study of Orientalism. Said's discussion of the mythographic dimensions of the relationship between East and West might also provide a viable linkage within Ambler between his early and later work. But first, Said's understanding of the representations of the East should be delineated.

In the matter of the approach to the Orient, Said avers that the European (and now American) cannot approach the East, either academically or commercially, with a neutral set of ideas or values, because the interests of countries in that part of the world stem from colonial relationships. Said defines the perspective of the Westerner who participates in the experience of the East at any level, albeit nonpolitical, as one that is originally and perpetually "tinged and impressed with, violated by, the gross political fact" as an epistemological event grounded in the power interests of the West (Said, 11). If, according to Said, the various ways of knowing the East are intrinsically tainted, Ambler's development of the Eurasian protagonist and narrator in the figure of Arthur Abdel Simpson, and later of Michael Howell in *The Levanter* (1972), is an accurate concession to the divestment of ethnocentrism in this cluster of novels. Simpson may not be heroic, but he is authentic as a character and reliable as a narrator. Ambler's Oriental narrative conforms to the epistemological conditions of Said's critique; Ambler avoids the privileged and empowered point of view of the intrusive European.

In the matter of material, Said's discourse on the mythography of the East is equally relevant to the peculiar themes and earlier intellectual grounding of Ambler's prewar novels. Said's illuminating comments may also explain Ambler's lifelong orientation (literally, to the East) toward the Balkans and beyond. Said defines the mystique of the East:

> The Orient is not only adjacent to Europe; it is also the place of Europe's greatest and richest and oldest colonies, the source of its civilizations and languages, its cultural contestant, and one of its deepest and most recurring images of the Other. In addition, the Orient has helped to define

> Europe (or the West) as its contrasting image, idea, personality, experience. . . .
>
> [This book] tries to show that European culture gained in strength and identity by setting itself off against the Orient as a sort of surrogate and even underground self. (1, 3)

Much of my own analysis of the Ambler canon in this present critique has adopted a related perspective that Ambler, through the appropriation of the Jungian apparatus of depth psychology, was working toward an evaluative statement on the Apollonian culture and comportment of the West. Aided by his readings in Nietzsche and Spengler, Ambler found a powerful undercurrent of textual meanings in the modern confrontation of the isolated self that "bumps into the Shadow"—the unconscious and mysterious (and Eastern) source of the unrecognized self. As stated in the treatment of earlier works in previous chapters of this study, Ambler worked through several versions of the Dionysian spirit and its eternal return in various characters (and villains) in his early novels. Hence, using the commentary of Edward Said, the Ambler reader might well connect, as Ambler himself may have done in his reading of the postwar "interior world," the later themes and materials of the Oriental novels to the Dionysiac motif of the early Ambler.

In his Oriental novels, Ambler moves to the symbolic formulation that "the light of the European day" is the radiant dawn of the Oriental daybreak—and it is the double dawn of civilization and consciousness. Eric Ambler's literary critique of the smug superiority of the West is founded on his own (remember his following the Oriental mystic Gurdjieff in Paris) recognition of the Orwellian adumbration. The latter had hinted unequivocally that the intellectual and moral honesty of taking historical inquiry into authentic Dionysian sources involved a long journey to the East. Ambler transcended the Orwellian lead by tapping back into the underpinnings of the apparatus of the collective unconscious.

The telltale signifier of Ambler's deep structure and design for *The Light of Day* can be found in its frontispiece maps, which show the route of Miss Lipp's car from central Italy to Istanbul. More graphically, the maps in each instance depict the splitting of Asia from Europe and the cleft of Istanbul itself across the Bosphorus. The maps underscore the thematic and structural bifurcation of the novel and its double-heritaged hero, Simpson. For Ambler, the maps locate and fix the *axis mundi* of the intricate design of Eurasian history and culture, and at the same time Ambler has found an outward model of the Jungian bicameral mind. The prepossessive and arrogant consciousness of the European ego at this synapse bumps up against the Dionysian and Asian unconscious. For Ambler, and later for Said, the encounter of the Westerner with the essence of Orientalism is a bit like the ancient Semitic proverb: "The anvil outlasts the hammer." Ambler is on the side of the anvils.

Dirty Story

Arthur Abdel Simpson's second novel (punctuated by the 1964 *A Kind of Anger*), *Dirty Story,* was found by many critics to be dull and unsavory. The novel's British publisher, Bodley Head, complained that the book sold poorly (Wolfe, 168). Nevertheless, *Dirty Story* progresses along a thematic continuum in which Ambler interrogates the Western (and capitalist, in this novel) bias encapsulated in Orientalism. The deep structure of the novel, in fact, employs a graphic illustration that betrays the central theme and image of the age-old "dirty story" (used extensively by Ambler in his early novels) of the driving force of greed and commerce in the misery of war. Before the examination of this structural and thematic element in an otherwise thin and somewhat dissatisfying novel, a discussion of the book's "dirty stories" should provide a background to the analytical exploration.

In examining this sequel to *The Light of Day* (subtitled *A Further Account of the Life and Adventures of Arthur Abdel Simpson*), the Ambler reader might recall that the "dirty stories" revolving around Simpson originate in his British schooling. In *The Light of Day,* Simpson had recalled his near termination at Coram's, the public school to which his father's military pension had sent him, because he had distributed and sold copies of a dirty poem. Ironically, the voyeuristic scenario of the adolescent poem is vividly enacted in real life many years later when Simpson is ensnared to participate in the Topkapi heist and forced by circumstances to witness the amours of Harper and Miss Lipp.

At the beginning of *Dirty Story,* Simpson is back at home in Athens and still wrestling with his old problem of nationality and ownership of an active British passport. In the pathetic opening scene, Simpson is being lectured mercilessly by a priggish British embassy figure who bluntly informs Simpson: "You're a disgusting creature, Mr. Simpson. Your life is nothing but a long, dirty story."[6] With great sarcasm,

Ambler implicitly defends his character in the course of the one-sided, power-heavy conversation by showing that the arm of the residual British Empire has no difficulty ignoring the circumstances of Simpson's dual heritage. Because his British father and Egyptian mother did not officially marry and because his father died in the war, Arthur was recognized as a war orphan but never qualified for British citizenship. Thus, even in the mid-1960s, at the time of the sequel, and even after Simpson's cooperation with the Turkish authorities in the Topkapi affair, Simpson continues a scrubby and raffish existence on the outer margins of legal and moral conduct.

Denied a British passport at the consulate, Simpson initiates a process to secure a "passport of convenience" from a country such as Panama or Costa Rica, which can usually be purchased in the byways and back streets of Athens. Haphazardly, Simpson orders a passport but lacks the means to pay for it. Hence, the Greek middleman for the passport proposes a barter; Simpson will simply work off the cost of the passport by providing certain services for an Italian film operation. Simpson soon learns that his chauffeur and guide services are being used by a pornographic film company that needs a cast for its productions.

Simpson's hiring of "actresses" runs afoul of an established Athenian brothel and its proprietor, Madame Irma. Monsieur Hayek, the film's director and producer, informs Simpson that the movies will follow a classical precedent and emulate Dionysiac orgies and mysteries. Even Simpson can spot unbelievable depravity and realizes he is embroiled in another dirty story. When the film crew encourages the actresses to leave the brothel, Madame Irma calls in the police. Both Simpson and his newfound thuggish ally, Goutard, flee Greece on a night freighter to Port Said. Goutard, a former French paratrooper and mercenary, befriends Simpson when the latter uses his father's military expertise as his own. Goutard believes Simpson to be a fellow soldier of fortune, and this false identity leads Simpson into the underworld of the dirty little wars of the Third World.

When the ship vibrates into shuddering disrepair in Djibouti, Goutard and Simpson are literally stranded on an African beach. Enter Jean Batiste Kinck—a procurement agent for European commercial interests in "rare earth" mining. Kinck explains that "rare earth" ores and deposits are in demand for nuclear arms production. Kinck will strike Ambler readers at this juncture as a Simon Groom in the tropics—different uniform on the same merchant of death. Kinck claims to be looking for "security personnel"; later, much too late for Simpson, it becomes obvious that Simpson has been recruited for a mercenary force that will grab ore-rich territory for an unnamed African equatorial republic. What Simpson does not, and cannot, know is that an equally well-armed force of white mercenaries has been raised by the other side; both sides have been manipulated by multinational European consortia that are writing the script of the ultimate dirty story in the novel. The real winners will be the nonnative commercial interests who instigated a war so that a peaceful resolution will ensure the practice of "business as usual": the extraction of ore and the manufacture of high-tech weapon components. For Ambler, this level of meaning in *Dirty Story* marks a return to the old anticapitalist position of the novels of the 1930s. In 1967, surely the news from Vietnam figured in Ambler's repertoire of themes—the dirty little wars of postcolonial Asia and the eager readiness of the arms merchants.

Although it takes place in equatorial Africa, *Dirty Story* is in many ways a Vietnam tale. For Ambler, it is also, finally, a war story—coming oddly enough twenty-two years after his involvement in a very different World War II. The whole second half of the book is a graphic description of jungle guerrilla warfare in a skein of scenes that could easily reflect the televised images of Vietnam on the evening news. In this perspective, *Dirty Story* fits into the cluster of Asian novels.

Simpson descends into the underground hell of a dirty little war. Two fictional African countries, Mahindi and Ugazi, are involved in a trivial border dispute that escalates into an armed standoff at the frontier when both countries realize that the contested areas are rich in "rare earth" ore deposits. The backdrop of the neocolonial incursion is an Edenic jungle that is "half steam bath and half oven" (124). The "rare earth" itself is a preternatural landscape scarred by the mechanical intrusion of the industrial age. The aerial view afforded Simpson when the plane descends is a pastoral vision of lush landscape under assault from the mechanical scourge of Western outsiders:

> At first the country below looked like a lot of dark-green moss without distinguishable features. Then as we got lower I could see that what I was looking at were tree-covered hills. Suddenly the green was broken by a series of long red gashes which converged on a sprawl of big shed-like buildings connected by dirt tracks. There was earth-moving machinery working there and a contraption that looked like a giant hose. A long fat jet of dirty water spouted from it into the red hillside. (131)

The blood-red laceration of the green "rare earth" represents both the effects of colonization (even in the hands of multinational consortia) and the old Ambler Marxian statement of the dialectic opposition between nature and culture. The earth-moving equipment is the machine in the Third World garden, perpetrating a violent act of displacement that provides an analogy for terrible dislocations of human scale in the military-industrial complex's dirty business.

In the novel's central image and theme, the "rare earth" itself is rendered by Ambler in an illustration that succinctly and symbolically encapsulates the essence of the "dirty story." A simple drawing in the novel (on page 141) depicts the "dirt," or "rare earth," that is the contested ground of ore deposits between the two countries. Kinck demonstrates this design to his new mercenary recruits and says sardonically: "Rather like a dollar sign, isn't it?" (140). The dollar sign is indeed the *axis mundi* of this patch of rare earth, by which the colonial and commercial industrial world has rendered the original design of nature into a "dirty story" of greed, violence, and racism. The *s* part of the design is the original border cut by a natural river; the vertical slash is the political frontier created by the intrusion of the old French colonial interests. Now, in the era of rare-earth mining, the neocolonial commercial designs are to wreak havoc on both sides through an artificial war. The resultant peace treaty will eradicate all old lines and establish, poetically, a dollar-sign-like neutrality in which business as usual will emerge. The real rulers of the dollar-sign republic are foreign commerce and corrupt native politicians. Of course, the invisible rulers are also the producers of the nuclear weapons made possible by the mining of that bit of rare earth. The atomic dirt is at the heart of the macrocosmic "dirty story" that envelops all the lesser stories and adventures of Arthur Abdel Simpson.

Simpson not only survives the imbroglio in the jungle war underworld but also emerges from the affair with sixteen passports. He takes them in passage to Tangier, where he sells eleven for handsome prices. He will return to Athens and his wife, Nicki, in fine fettle. Most interestingly, Peter Wolfe has characterized Simpson's survival as the triumph of the Dionysian: "The structure of *Story* invokes Nietzsche's doctrine of eternal recurrence" (164). Simpson's rascality is an alternate mask of the more deadly insinuations of the reptilian Dimitrios; echoes of the orgiastic song of the Bacchantes may indeed be a "dirty story," but the will to power from its antique Asian source is evident even in the raffish and peripheral existence of Simpson's Oriental soul.

The Levanter

Taking place during the tumultuous events in the eastern Mediterranean in 1971, *The Levanter,* the last of the five Oriental novels, explores the explosive territorial dispute between Palestinians and Israelis. Focusing on Syria and Lebanon, the title hearkens back to the etymology of the "Levant"—the eastern realm of the "rising" (*lever* in French) of the sun. Thus, *The Levanter* reflects the same "light of day" theme in which the Orient's dawn of civilization is encapsulated in the diurnal breaking of day. Significantly, the climactic action of *The Levanter* moves mythopoetically in a night-sea journey toward the East, in which the nocturnal descent into the near-death of the night sea is transformed and drawn upward to the "rising sun" of new day and new life.

The Levanter renders a resonantly new variation of the old Ambler motif of the survival of a strangely innocent and pure Dionysiac spirit in the lethal clutter of greed, treachery, and violence. This latter-day Dionysus (much like his 1939 predecessor, Dimitrios) is not without artifice and chicanery; in this novel he is the titular character, Michael Howell, a Levanter, who (like Arthur Simpson) is a double-heritaged hero prepossessed of those virtuous and villainous qualities that constitute the trickster in his eternal return. Like his generic ancestor of epic Greece, Michael Howell also invokes another linguistic meaning from the title; like Odysseus, he travels and trades his stock of rascality on the seafaring ships of the Levant.

Also like Odysseus, the modern-day Levanter is an accomplished singer of epic song—the "stitcher of odes" in that traditional bardic vein. Facile of mind and tongue, Michael Howell additionally possesses the heroic traits of physical cunning and mechanical aptitude—like Ambler himself, Howell was trained as an engineer in a red-brick and lackluster polytechnic school "in one of the grimier parts of London."[7] Somewhat akin to Arthur Simpson, Howell absorbs the "dirty story" of a Levantine "mongrel" in academic circles of the British public school. But Howell immediately surpasses the tawdry penchants of Simpson, taking up the demanding and treacherous tasks of his family's maritime trade and transport business consortium in the eastern Mediterranean. In Michael Howell, Ambler reaches fruition in his literary fracturing of traditional Orientalism; Howell is the apotheosis of the double-heritaged hero whose consciousness is conceived from within, a modern literary character whose actions and values are formed beyond the suspicion and prejudice found "under Western eyes."

The last in a long line of Ambler's engineers as main characters, Howell has transcended by light years the wooden and monolithic consciousness of *The Dark Frontier*'s amnesiac Barstow and all of his fellow prewar technicians. In the mediation of Western and Eastern forces, Ambler has created in Howell, the Levanter, a dual-heritaged hero who combines and mediates the oppositional dialectics of the Occident and the Orient. The Levanter is the personification of the Nietzschean superman, who by dint of modern engineering skills and ancient survival skills overcomes the extremes of the East-West schism and depicts a viable center of mediation. Howell shares the primeval instincts of Dimitrios, but his more immediate predecessor in the Ambler canon is the *Fallschirmjager,* the modern paratrooper deus ex machina of an updated Greek religious drama and comedy, Franz Schirmer.

Like *The Schirmer Inheritance, The Levanter* begins with a lengthy prelude on the history of the novel's focus, this time on the Palestinian-Israeli conflict. The novel has three different narrators: the American journalist Lewis Prescott, who tells the first, third, and last chapters; Michael Howell, who delivers four chapters; and Teresa Malandra, Howell's Italian assistant and mistress, who narrates a tender and trenchant fifth chapter at the center of the novel. The variations embedded in this multivalent narrative underscore the complexity of the central character and the ambient issues of politics, greed, and commerce in the eastern Mediterranean. In the narrative, no one perspective ensures the reliability of its own or any other text; in the character of Michael Howell, no one persona ensures familiarity or knowledge of the total person. Howell's multidimensional personality recalls Ambler's earlier inclusion of Jungian depth psychology and also provides an ambiguous but accurate admixture of Western and Eastern character traits. His multiple layers form the focus of the chapter revealed by Malandra. Howell is the apotheosis of the hybrid, dual-heritaged hero who represents the destruction by Ambler of a genre's long history of restrictive Orientalism.

The first eighty pages of *The Levanter* furnish background information on the postcolonial history of the Levant and its resultant "homeland" dilemma for Arabs and Jews. The focus of the novel's activities is Syria, although Beirut and Cyprus are on the periphery. At the end of the story, Israel also figures as a presence and a place. Prescott and Howell deliver much of the prefatory information. Ambler's use of different perspectives helps avoid a prejudicial point of view; in fact, Howell the Levanter is capable of a real ambivalence in expressing his sympathies. Ambler and his three narrators walk a fine but balanced line as only a dilemma, not a cause, is presented.

The convergence of two key characters, Howell and a Palestinian guerrilla leader, Salah Ghaled, reflects in microcosm the larger conflict between Palestinian liberation groups and Israel over the right to a homeland and an independent national state. The early narrative episodes of *The Levanter* portray poignantly and economically the parallel but quite different tracks of the education and maturation of two sons of the Levant—one the son of Palestinian refugees and the other the scion of a wealthy and formerly colonial family. It is in part the old tale of the prince and the pauper—but this time told from within the Middle Eastern labyrinth.

The colonial-derived prince and the colonial-deprived pauper are inadvertently linked when the prince (Howell) sets up a series of manufacturing industries in Syria and one of those factories is subverted by the pauper for the assembly of terrorist bombs. When Howell and Malandra accidentally stumble upon the nocturnal operation at their Green Circle battery plant, they suddenly find themselves at the mercy of their "employees," whom they now know to be a splintered and violent faction of Al Fatah, a principal Palestinian liberation front. This particular cell of the splinter force is preparing to mount a major terrorist assault on Israel; sitting in the plant manager's chair, Salah Ghaled informs Howell that all of the high-tech explosives to be used in the operation are being assembled in the battery plant.

Ghaled gives Howell and Malandra a simple choice: if they wish to leave the factory alive, they will immediately sign an oath of loyalty to the Palestinian cause. The oath entails a barbed snag; it says nothing of loyalty to the PLO but instead states that both are agents of Zionist intelligence services who are engaged in the transport of arms and explosives. Howell and Malandra are thereby forced to support the Palestinians. The Howell family conglomerate of maritime and manufacturing businesses is in one fell swoop aligned with both the Palestinian and Israeli causes. Howell can be victimized and accused easily by either side, if and when Ghaled should choose. The Levanter is trapped by an intricate Levantine design.

Like Odysseus, Michael Howell goes to his island home in the Mediterranean (Cyprus) and plots an equally convoluted plan that will restore the welfare of his family and kingdom—the mighty shipping business of the Levant. Also like the Homeric hero, Howell utilizes the craft of camouflage and his innate sense of timing—stealthy operations on the open sea are his stock-in-trade—and he waits.

As the operational moment approaches, Ghaled informs Howell of the main outline of the entire assault. The explosives assembled in the machine shop of Howell's Syrian factory are only a minor chord in a major concerto. The small bombs will be detonated all over Israel as a diversion in advance of the major thrust of the attack. Ghaled and his confederates plan to bring two ships within striking distance of Tel Aviv and to bombard the city's seafront with a barrage of deadly missiles launched from the seaborne platforms. Howell's ships are integrally involved with this plan, and Ghaled's invasion of Howell's maritime homecourt eventually dooms the terrorist attack. Howell manages to get Ghaled to allow him on the command ship on the night of the attack, and the maritime master is able to orchestrate his counterattack on the Palestinian terrorists.

Much of the excitement in *The Levanter* comes not from the machinations of this storyline; instead, Ambler establishes a vital center by creating an intense relationship between the two sons of the Levant. The game is that of cat and mouse, and each player is capable of enormous chicanery and the old Amblerian art of reptilian camouflage. Each revelation in the unfolding drama of the terrorist assault is matched by the clever and subtle cunning of Howell's engineering savvy and instinctual homing in on survival. Ambler's study, in the form of Teresa Malandra's appraisal, of the complexity of Howell's mind and persona is reminiscent of his earlier use of Jungian psychology.

As a rare female narrator in the Ambler canon, Malandra delivers an unusual and poignant chapter. It is in the eye of the novel's storm and provides a putative appraisal of her boss and lover, Michael Howell. Malandra opens her narrative with a paean to Howell:

> The reason why Michael is so difficult to understand— especially for journalists—is that he is not one person but a committee of several. There is, for instance, the Greek money-changer with thin fingers moving unceasingly as he makes lightning calculations on an abacus; there is the brooding, sad-eyed Armenian bazaar trader who pretends to be slow-witted, but is, in fact, devious beyond belief; there is the stuffy, no-nonsense Englishman trained as an engineer; there is the affable, silk-suited young man of affairs with smile lines at the corners of wide, limpid, con-man eyes; there is the mother-fixated managing director of the Agency Howell, defensive, sententious, and given to speechifying; and there is

> one I particularly like, who . . . but why go on? The Michael Howell committee is in permanent session, and, though the task of implementing its business decisions is generally delegated to just one of the members, the voices of the others are usually to be heard whispering in the background. Ghaled certainly detected the faint sounds of those prompting voices, but to begin with he positively identified only the engineer. About that member of the committee, at least, his judgment was correct; the Englishman's professional pride borders on the obsessional. (127–28)

Malandra's description of Howell represents an act of love; it also indicates a deep resignation to the fact of the inscrutability of the archetypal Levanter. Michael Howell is portrayed in the multiple personae of a "Middle Eastern committee" of which Dimitrios the fig-packer might once have been part. The difference between Howell and Dimitrios is that the stench of the primeval swamp, part of Dimitrios's makeup, has been deodorized in the Amblerian notion of the twentieth century's transformation. By 1971, Ambler had come to terms with the unexpected survival of civilization—the apocalyptic jeremiads of Nietzsche and Spengler had not come to pass. To be sure, capitalist greed and the big business of war were not ameliorated in the Ambler reshuffle; what happened was that Ambler came to recognize the perennial return of the Dionysiac in the mutability of the Franz Schirmers and Arthur Abdel Simpsons. The protean trickster is a heroic spirit who returns to win the day, not a cataclysmic revolutionary who levels everything to ground zero.

Dimitrios dies by the violence that he personally practiced; Ghaled suffers the same fate in *The Levanter.* Michael Howell is a brother to Franz Schirmer, and committed to the latter's instinct for self-preservation in the modern jungle of boardrooms and courtrooms. Howell is a portrait of the Dionysiac con artist as a young organization man. The Jungian shadow now sits as a committee, like a board of directors ruling over the complex and multiple functions of the psyche. In Michael Howell, the Jungian shadow has been located in its Oriental genesis. Ambler finally gets it right: the stuffy English engineer with a flair for survival who constitutes a harmonious blending of East and West. And the wily Ambler has pretty much taken in the reader near the end of the novel by staying with a violence-purged hero in Howell. And then, in one of Ambler's most triumphant literary scenes, the final episode of the novel contains an interview with all three narrators present.

Prescott interviews Howell, and Teresa Malandra is there as well. Prescott is curious about the circumstances of Ghaled's being shot and killed—apparently by Howell on the ship at the moment of interception by the Israeli navy. Prescott asks Howell the question point-blank:

> "Did you kill Salah Ghaled?"
>
> He thought about it for a moment and then smiled. "Teresa says that sometimes I am not one man but a committee. Why don't we ask her?" He turned his smile in her direction. "Teresa, my dear, have you ever noticed among the committee members a murderer?"
>
> She returned the smile, but I thought that there was an appraising look in her eyes. "No, Michael. No, I can't say that I've ever seen a murderer."
>
> "There is your answer, Mr. Prescott." (242)

In a brilliant tour de force, Ambler pulls the ideological carpet out from under the unsuspecting reader. In a sudden rush on the membership of the corporate boardroom, Dimitrios returns in a swift entry and takes a vacant seat. The seat was still warm, for a laughing Franz Schirmer knew that he was expected. The committee was whole again.

The achievement of Eric Ambler's five Eastern novels lies in proximity to his accomplishment in the six novels he produced on the eve of World War II. Ambler created a world in his fiction that he saw prefigured in the contemporary mind and manners of both periods. In the late 1930s, Ambler reproduced a world bent on its own destruction; in the 1950s and 1960s, Ambler represented a Western world involved in Southeast Asia and later, when the oil embargo developed, in the Middle East. In this latter clutch of novels, Ambler inherited the view from Orwell and Conrad that suggested the traditional Western gaze had missed much of the spirit and spirituality of the East. These latter qualities may well be termed the mysticism of the Orient. Eric Ambler had been attracted to it as a young man in Paris in the late 1920s. Even as he explored Jung, Nietzsche, and Spengler in this period, the young Ambler had a deep fascination with the mystical Gurdjieff—a former fig-packer whose story shares many similarities with that of another refugee from Smyrna.

When the conflagration forecast by Nietzsche and Spengler did not materialize, the Jungian apparatus became the sole surviving dialectic from the prewar novels. Ambler then tracks the Jungian shadow back to its Byzantine origins. The coalescence of the Jungian motif of "bumping into one's Shadow, or Other" with the investigation of the Orient by the empirical observer/engineer/journalist is the driving force of this later cluster of novels. Ambler intuitively transposed the spiritual tragedy of Conrad's colonial and imperial "heart of darkness" to the larger canvas of the existential tragedy of the postcolonial unleashing of the Bacchantes. Western Pentheus would be destroyed again.

Chapter Seven

Ambler Redux: Fruition and Finale

What must be fairly obvious by now should nevertheless be stated: Eric Ambler transformed the literature of espionage in the 1930s and never again actually wrote a "spy story." Clearly, one factor in defining what Ambler did write must involve the distinction between fiction about professional spies and fiction in which ordinary people become entangled in a dangerous adventure that demands their engagement in espionage-like intrigue. If one accepts the boundaries of the latter, with uneven measures of philosophical and historical texts interwoven in the plot, one approximates the elusive and changeable formula achieved by Ambler.

A final element that Ambler worked into his formula is the theme of alienation. Along with Graham Greene and John Le Carré, Ambler astutely foresaw and later shaped the conjunction of one of the principal motifs of modernism—alienation—with the spy novel: loneliness was a natural thematic graft onto the old, cumbersome vehicle of the spy story.

In 1964, at the same time that Ambler finished *A Kind of Anger,* he edited the anthology *To Catch a Spy.* In the introduction he makes an interesting observation that perhaps escaped even his own considered reflection. He says: "Spying is lonely and often depressing work. The spy's friendships can only be warily professional. His appetites and weaknesses, even the small ones, must be rigidly self-controlled. He must be capable of living for long periods under exceptional nervous strain" (5). The corrosive despair and monumental alienation of the latter half of the twentieth century have surely found a means of expression in the literary milieu of espionage created by Ambler, Greene, and Le Carré. The lonely and dangerous gauntlets run by their introspective and doubt-ridden spies are the same corridors of deceit recognized in an everyday world beset by global and personal angst.

In his late 1950s essay, "The White Negro," Norman Mailer described the postatomic neurosis as being epitomized in the absolute freedom of the psychopath. Mailer accurately foresaw the culture of liberation that emerged in the 1960s because of the intensely personal, and at the same time universal, threat of annihilation. Mailer also described the despair and alienation that would accompany the breakout into liberational modes of existence. Eric Ambler recognized the same conditions. Having read his Nietzsche, Jung, and Spengler, Ambler knew well the risks attendant on the return of Dionysus and the sometimes psychopathic trickster.

The two final novels to be examined in this critique of the Ambler canon represent in various ways his final treatment of this persistent theme and subject. Piet Maas of *A Kind of Anger* (1964) and Theodore Carter of *The Intercom Conspiracy* (1969) are kindred spirits to the Amblerian trickster character; both novels, although not Ambler's last, represent the fruition and finale of his long encounter with the Nietzschean and Oriental principle of eternal return and transformation.

A Kind of Anger

This novel combines two of Ambler's most powerful and recurrent narrative and thematic devices: the journalist who moves from observer to participant and the transformation of the hero in an awakening to a dangerous and quickening Dionysiac consciousness. *A Kind of Anger* opens in New York on a late Friday night in February 1963. In the upper-management offices of the weekly news magazine *World Reporter,* the editor-in-chief, Mr. Cust, is preparing for his weekly ritual of making a harassing call to one of his unfortunate bureau chiefs. On this particular evening, Cust calls his chief in Paris, Sy Logan. Cust informs him of a hot lead on a murder case from the month before in Switzerland. An Iraqi exile named Arbil, a former military man living in Zurich, was mysteriously murdered and the only known witness, a woman in a bikini, had disappeared. The Swiss authorities had hit a dead end, and every magazine and newspaper in Western Europe was trying to find leads in the so-called "bikini murder." Cust had a tip from the U.S. Treasury Department, and he was calling to charge his Paris bureau with a long-shot mission. Sy Logan tries to fend off the assignment, but Cust wants Piet Maas, an employee Cust dislikes, to take on the job. Logan suspects Cust is really setting Maas up for failure and is worried about Maas's mental stability.

Piet Maas was born of a Rotterdam family. His parents were killed in that city's bombing during the war. Evacuated to London as an orphan, Maas was taken in by a business associate of his father and sent to an English school. Trained as a journalist, Maas became editor and part owner of an experimental international news review that ultimately went bankrupt. On the day his magazine failed, Maas came home early and found his live-in girlfriend in bed with another man. He soon afterward attempted suicide and then spent several months in a French mental hospital undergoing shock treatments. Following his convalescence, Maas was hired at *World Reporter* as a researcher. When he committed an error on an important story, Cust learned of his personal history and thereafter called him the "Dutch psycho." Maas, meanwhile, suffers from insomnia. Even sleeping pills do not work. He somewhat welcomes the Arbil assignment, which will take him away from the bureau and to the south of France. The French Riviera is Eric Ambler country.

The homicide occurred at the sumptuous Zurich residence of an Iraqi colonel in exile from the revolutionary Baghdad government. Colonel Ahmed Fathir Arbil had nearly four years earlier been in attendance at a Geneva conference when his government was shaken by an army revolt. Arbil asked the Swiss authorities for political asylum, and from that time forward had lived in Zurich. While an army intelligence chief, Arbil had been known as a sympathizer to the Kurdish nationalist movement. After taking up residence in Switzerland, Arbil professed to be working on a history of Kurdistan. He also developed an appetite for young, buxom, unmarried women. Thus, Lucia Bernardi entered his life. Arbil had met her at St. Moritz during the winter season, and she moved into his Zurich residence not long afterward. After Arbil's murder, the Swiss police found several photos of Bernardi posing in a bikini. She fled the house on the night of the murder, and the authorities had not been able to track her down.

The lead supplied by Cust to Piet Maas is this: at the time that Lucia Bernardi met Arbil in St. Moritz, she was working a confidence swindle on rich old men with a male partner calling himself Patrick Chase (his real name is Phillip Sanger). Cust has called the Paris bureau to tell them that Sanger could be found in Nice. Maas's job is to find Sanger and determine whether he is involved in hiding Bernardi.

When Maas arrives, in a cold February wind, at the deserted, out-of-season French coastal resort, luck initially eludes him. Then, in a café outside Nice, Maas discovers from the matron that Sanger and his wife live nearby. He drives his rental car right up to Sanger's elegantly secluded farmhouse. After at first being denied admission, Maas sends through the servant the name "Patrick Chase," the alias of Sanger. Maas is quickly ushered into Sanger's presence. After some artful dodging on Sanger's part, Maas lowers the boom: "You see, the person I'm interested in is

Lucia Bernardi. Not you, Mr. Sanger, not Patrick Chase. But if I can't get the story I want on Lucia Bernardi, I'll have to do the best I can with a story about all three of you."[1]

Sanger's facade quickly collapses, and he talks. He describes how he enlisted Lucia into a partnership of crime after finding her as a salesperson in a Paris shop. She was beautiful—and had a mind for numbers and money. Lucia and Sanger ran a scam in which wealthy older men would be led to believe that they had stolen the affections of another man's mistress. The scheming twosome haunted the summer and winter playgrounds of the wealthy. They found Colonel Arbil in St. Moritz. Arbil fell head over heels in love with Lucia. And then the first of a number of unlikely events took place: Lucia "after a few days took the tumble, too" (48). Sanger and Lucia dissolved their partnership, and Lucia became the mistress of the Arbil house in Zurich. And there she stayed until her flight on the night of the colonel's murder.

The question that Maas now poses for Sanger is the matter of Lucia's present whereabouts. Sanger describes Peira-Cava, a small town in the mountains above Nice, near the Italian frontier. Sanger tells of Lucia's memory of staying at a pension in Peira-Cava in the midst of winter when the heating system failed. Hot bricks were wrapped in newspaper and passed out to the guests. (This scenario also constitutes the opening passage of chapter 8 of *Here Lies;* in the same town and circumstances the young Eric Ambler had written *Cause for Alarm* in the winter of 1938.)

Piet Maas eventually finds Lucia Bernardi. But by the time he locates her, his quest is for more than a simple news magazine story. Maas admits to himself, on the way to his first meeting with her, "I had become interested in the mystery of Lucia Bernardi. I wanted to know what lay behind it, and I wanted to hear the truth from her own lips" (71).

Maas gets part of the story from Lucia, but his editor in Paris wants to run the larger story, which includes the role of Sanger and his wife, Adèle. Maas refuses, and when the editor threatens him, he hangs up the phone and decides to cut and run. When he goes to Sanger to warn him of the magazine's intention to print the whole story, Maas ends up throwing in with the Sangers and once again speaks to Lucia. Through the course of several conversations with Lucia, Maas begins to discover the truthful recesses of her story. Her account of Arbil's murder was accurate, but she omitted the fact that she had been able to take out of the house his briefcase full of secret papers. Arbil had anticipated his demise; the briefcase and its contents were to be Lucia's equity and insurance policy. The secret papers would command a monumental selling price from either the Italian oil concessionaires in Iraq or the Iraqi government. Lucia had had no means of protecting herself in dealing with these agents, but she finds a bodyguard in Maas.

But being bodyguard to a beautiful and treacherous woman is not enough for Piet Maas; he transforms completely in the Dionysiac tradition of the trickster. He proposes a deal to Lucia: "You have something to sell—a suitcase full of records, perhaps. But first you have to let the prospective buyers know that it is for sale. At the same time you have to be very careful not to let them know too much, or they might try to take it without paying" (130). Maas presents himself as her new business partner—and Lucia bursts out laughing. After the laughter subsides, their illegal partnership is effected, and soon another pact—that of the flesh—is consummated between the two fugitives from a nicer world.

As that outer and more refined world begins to get the picture of Maas's defection from the news magazine and his possible alliance with the missing "bikini woman," the news reports characterize Maas as an "unpredictable screwball." In the meantime, the "screwball" excels in the most dangerous game of selling national secrets to foreign powers. Maas exercises a natural talent for the big-time scam; he is trickster par excellence. Like Franz Schirmer, Maria Kolin, and Michael Howell, Piet Maas had dwelled temporarily in the land of the dead; at the wondrous moment of his rebirth into a full life of the senses, he returns from death with the gifts of prophecy, vision, and wholeness.

Phillip Sanger, as a sort of kindly godfather of rascality, foresees the transformation of Maas long before it happens. Sanger as the eminent high priest of crime and chicanery even seems to give his blessing to these godchildren about to unite in dubious criminality. When Maas first returns to the Sangers and tells them he has "defected" from the magazine, he seems to be basing his quarrel with the editors on some obscure "honor among thieves" principle. At this moment, Sanger asks Maas: "What is it with you, Maas? Self-destruction still, or is there a new kind of anger now?" (94). A few pages later, Sanger continues: "Lucia interests you and attracts you. So much so that you are prepared to cheat on your bosses to pursue the matter with her in your own way. That's your new kind of anger" (96–97). Sanger is a perceptive amateur psychologist, and his observations mark Ambler's return to the use of depth psychology (more Freud than Jung, in this case) in the depiction of the novice's convergence with the shadow, or the unconscious. Maas has traded Thanatos for Eros and undergoes a metamorphosis that is aptly described by Sanger at the novel's conclusion.

When Sanger and his wife join Maas and Lucia at the conclusion of the scam and the novel (actually the Sangers join in, for a fee, the successful finale of extorting from all sides), Sanger confides in Maas as all four partners-in-crime relish their triumph:

> "Have you any idea, any idea at all, my friend, how much you have changed during the last few days?"
>
> "I've had other things to think about," I said impatiently. "I still have."
>
> He took no notice. "When one compares," he went on, wide-eyed with amazement, "the brooding young man with the haunted eyes and the aura of death, the man who sat in this very room a week ago apologizing for the iniquity of his existence—when one compares that man with the arch conspirator hunted by the police, who risks assassination by hired gunmen and makes daring, ingenious plans to sell secrets to the representatives of a foreign power, one can only . . ." He broke off, overcome again by helpless laughter. (232)

Maas tries to protest and explain the transformation by the change of circumstances. But Sanger is too keen an observer of human nature:

> "Oh, no," he said when he could speak again. "Oh no, that's not the answer. I thought I knew what made you tick. 'A new kind of anger,' I said. How wrong I was! Your kind of anger is as old as the hills. You've just bottled it up all these years—just like the man who becomes a policeman instead of a crook. Or is that sublimation? It doesn't matter. The point is that you have a taste for larceny. It agrees with you. Therapy!" He started to giggle. "Instead of giving you all those shock treatments, you know what they should have done? They should have sent you out to rob a bank!" (232–33)

Ambler might have his characters speak of "sublimation," and perhaps even demonstrate through Maas the substitution of Eros for Thanatos, but Ambler has not quite deserted the Jungian psychological terrain for Freud. Piet Maas is the apotheosis of the Apollonian hero who transmogrifies into the opposite—the Ambler character who enacts the Nietzschean drama of the "destruction of the old self and the rebirth of the Dionysiac." Piet Maas is the culmination of a long line of Ambler protagonists who epitomize the Nietzschean (and later Jungian) conflict between the rational and irrational forces that determine the psychosocial makeup of an age.

Significantly, the name of Maas's failed news review was *Ethos.* This word later becomes the password in maintaining the secrecy of his newfound profession; Phillip Sanger appreciates the irony of the term. An "ethos" is the spirit (or "geist" in Nietzschean and Jungian parlance) of a people, a civilization, or a system as expressed in its culture and institutions. From the equivalent Nietzschean and Jungian perspectives, the ethos is the dominant domain of regulatory behavior in a culture or an individual; that dominance is vulnerable to the shifting forces of the conflict between oppositional elements. For Nietzsche, the macrocosmic was always attempting to balance between the Apollonian and the Dionysian; for Jung, the battleground was the microcosmic psyche, attuned to the ethos, which was caught in the balancing of conscious and unconscious images and drives.

As discussed in appraising the earlier Ambler novels, Ambler was informed and fascinated by Nietzsche's philosophy and Jung's psychology. Ambler intuited correctly as a young thinker and writer that both systems of thought would be useful agencies for the assessment of the twentieth century and its interior and exterior battlegrounds. Slowly and gradually, Ambler's main characters through the course of most of the novels find their way to an experience like that of Piet Maas in *A Kind of Anger.* Some of the early characters discover their "opposite selves" through the authorial manipulation of amnesia and other altered states of consciousness; others merely witness and approximate the wondrous transformation of the Jungian *enantiodromia,* the process of "running contrariwise," of the larger Nietzschean notion that "sooner or later everything runs into its opposite." Thus, Latimer descends into the underworld of shadows in the Istanbul morgue, and really bumps into the shadow of his unconscious. Thus, George Carey descends into the asphyxiating cellar of legal tomes and finds a resurrection in the third month of a quest that ends on an obscure acadian mountain in mythical Macedonia.

Piet Maas, like his namesake river in the Netherlands, has the alternate spelling—Meuse—and an alternate direction. (He also has an alternate identifiable self.) Ambler's pun (based on his impeccable geographical knowledge) connotes the discovery of the self's muse—and the wondrous *enantiodromia* of the running to opposites and the Dionysiac following of the Orphic muse that leads upward toward the regenerative light (Lucia) of day. Piet Maas is the avatar of the trickster; when the prevalent ethos fails, he changes direction and pursues the shadow.

As an added bonus, Maas finds a kindred soul-shadow in Lucia (the light; also linguistically cognate to Lucifer). It is a marriage made in the primordial images of Jung and Nietzsche. And the high priest of the nuptial is the ceremonious Phillip Sanger. If the wedding has already been consummated in pacts of the wit and the flesh, Sanger is equal to ratifying the ritual vows: "You see, it is as I said. He has a natural talent for these affairs. You should be very happy together" (239). Not since the Orphic rescue of Maria Kolin by Franz Schirmer has a connubial prospect looked so promising.

Franz Schirmer's final words to George Carey may shed some symbolic illumination on Piet Maas's metamorphosis. In the letter left behind for Carey, after Schirmer and Kolin have absconded to Macedonia, Schirmer says he is able to relinquish his rightful inheritance only because he has received a gift of greater value: "My true inheritance is the knowledge you have brought me of my blood and of myself" (196–97). Maas's essential discovery is also one of the blood; the hint is in the name of the sacerdotal godfather who has united the wedded couple. Phillip Sanger's very name implies the French *la sangue,* the blood of a figurative consanguinity and extended family to which Piet Maas finds his trickster's way home. The Sangers are the new family for Maas and Lucia; their legacy would be easily recognized by the Schirmer family.

The final bit of significant imagery that informs this critical approach to Ambler in general and *A Kind of Anger* in particular is the anomalous scene near the very end. The two adoptive children in the Sanger family are clearly Maas and Lucia. The portrayal of the two initiates into the family as childlike innocents is necessary not only for the familial imagery but also because of Ambler's deep and abiding knowledge of Jung. In *Symbols of Transformation,* Jung has described the surrender to the unconscious through the agency of the libido as a regressive and infantile reverie. Jung states clearly: "For if he [any person] allows his libido to get stuck in a childish milieu, and does not free it for higher purposes, he falls under the spell of unconscious compulsion" (414). And Jung adds quickly, this "compulsion" was the "psychological situation of late antiquity," and the real purpose of all the mystery religions was to free humanity from the bondage of "compulsion by the stars." Jung quotes Frazer at length at this point in his text, and avers that all of the symbolism of death and rebirth illuminated the ancient Mediterranean rituals of initiation into the mysteries. This ritual death and resurrection, according to Jung, marked the individual's return to the balanced and full life of the body and the psyche, the healthy mediation of the conscious and the unconscious.

Ambler pays homage to both Jung and Frazer in a curiously bucolic scene at the end of *A Kind of Anger,* a scene reminiscent of the resolution of the arcadian and prelapsarian union of Franz Schirmer and Maria Kolin. When Maas and Lucia go to a house in Cagnes to retrieve the suitcase full of saleable secrets, they must approach the house, which is under surveillance, from a back garden, an olive grove presented in an arcadian setting. Maas and Lucia enter an ancient and mythical world on their way to the fabulous mysteries and fortunes that await:

> It was all very quiet there, but the olive grove possessed a special stillness of its own. The trees were old, and the light breeze did not move their thick, twisted limbs. Only the leaves moved, fluttering softly. Once, as we walked up, the black shape of a goat stirred, and the chain that tethered it made a clicking noise. Then, the bulk of the cistern loomed ahead and there was a sound of trickling water. A moment or two later, we had found the path. (218)

This pastoral portrait conveys the connubial criminals into a mythic space—a prelapsarian Eden. It is the combined age-old idyll of escape to a primeval garden and a wedding in the woods. The two orphans of a ruthless and Apollonian world have retreated back into the Dionysiac sanctuary—outside of time, place, and the law. Fiendishly capable, they are self-sufficient and find their only family in their true blood-relations with the Sangers and each other.

But, of course, they do have other blood. Somewhat to the east, in the imaginary frontier of Macedonia, are their first cousins in the family known as trickster, Franz and Maria. The fortuitous human pairings, emergent from the common themes between *The Schirmer Inheritance* and *A Kind of Anger,* allow the two connubial couples to inhabit the dark/bright, amoral frontier, suspended between good and evil, fixed between childhood and the inevitable.

The Intercom Conspiracy

After a lapse of exactly thirty years, Charles Latimer reappeared in *The Intercom Conspiracy* (1969). The novel attains an innovative style of narrative, suspense, and characterization; it even surpasses Ambler's previous novels in its experimentation with a Conradian point of view. But gone is the undercurrent philosophy of history. In lieu of a search for a logic in history, Ambler renders history at its face value. And history in this case is the cold war reality of two superpowers who must both seek a rapprochement in order to maintain a balance of power (even if it means conspiring together to maintain a balance of terror).

The Intercom Conspiracy is, however, not straight cold war plot. The spark of Ambler's old ingenuity becomes evident when Latimer stumbles on the extortion of the United States and Russia by a pair of NATO intelligence chiefs, Colonel Brand and Colonel Jost. Both superpowers are willing to stop the leakage of information by paying a handsome ransom and thereby preserve the equilibrium of power and access to intelligence. Ambler reveals the plot through the eyes of the innocent victim (not Latimer this time, though), and the whole method of discovery is still presented in terms of deductive detection. Ambler's sui generis formula has resurfaced along with his basic detective-novel approach: the "trapped innocent" enters the cold war.

The Intercom Conspiracy depicts the final, utter failure of the detective hero in the modern era of cold war espionage. Latimer is no match for the two traitorous NATO confederates; he is liquidated and silenced forever. The modern, corporate "organization" is both hero and villain in the cold war setting of "bloc" versus "bloc." There is really nothing heroic in Brand's and Jost's plot to blackmail the superpowers; they are merely successful bureaucrats who possess intimate knowledge of the innermost workings of big organizations:

> Jost and Brand came to power in the early nineteen-fifties and established themselves in the NATO intelligence community during the bitter cold-war years of that decade. . . .
>
> They could accept the necessity for the alliance to which their countries were committed. They could accept with resignation the knowledge that their countries meant no more to NATO than Romania or Bulgaria meant to the Warsaw Pact and that they were pygmies involved in a struggle between giants. What they could not do was change their ways of thinking about giants.
>
> They had known the German giant, so omnipotent in his day, and had helped to bring him down. Now, they were able to observe and appraise from peculiar vantage points the American and Russian giants. The appraisals they made were not flattering. What impressed them

> most about these giants, they ultimately decided, was not their strength, still less the loud and threatening noises they made, but their inherent clumsiness.[2]

The bureaucratic spies are successful because of their cognizance of organizational weaknesses. Their guarded daring is always protected by transactions through Swiss banks and telegrams. The personal confrontation of heroic encounter is absent.

Latimer's failure and death pose finally the ethical dilemma of the observer of history—one either observes at the Apollonian distance or one incurs a fatal set of consequences to active participation. For Ambler, the choice is quite basic, yet is as old as the Platonic dialogues and as awe-inspiring as Hamlet's soliloquy. Is history the product of an ineluctable process of events, or is there a morality of action that demands participation by the individual in the flux of society. Perhaps the solution lies in the very birth of the spy novel. It shows a complex world where the putative logician can no longer solve the riddle of the Sphinx. But there is the eternal rub—was Oedipus the logical detective or the political man of action? Either way, the result was self-destruction. This is the crucial dilemma of Eric Ambler's novels in one half of a divided stream in which Latimer's return and demise betray the failure of the Apollonian interventionist—the putative logician, last in a long line of Amblerian engineers, journalists, and technicians.

The other half of the divided stream of Ambler's protagonists is the "progeny" of survivors—the tricksters who slough off the Apollonian shell and emerge through a Dionysiac rebirth and transformation in an ebullient and amoral mode of pure existence. If *The Intercom Conspiracy* encapsulates the end of the Latimer line of descendancy, the character of Theodore Carter represents the survival of the scion of the Schirmer and Maas genealogy.

In some ways, Latimer is the least important of three primary character clusters. Latimer is present at the periphery, and never actually in person. Theodore Carter is a foil to Latimer's uninformed innocence. The two NATO colonels—Brand and Jost—form the third element of character study. Each of these characters has a distinctive voice and a role in the polydimensional narrative structure and tonality. For good reason Peter Wolfe writes about this novel: "Written mostly in the relaxed cadences of speech, it moves in tone from the colloquial to the digressive or the emotional, creating an impromptu, polyphonic effect that makes the telling of the story as vital as the story itself" (170).

Peter Lewis agrees that *Conspiracy* is "arguably the most innovative" of all of Ambler's novels (153). The complex nature of Ambler's final triumph lies specifically in the conflation of his two canonical themes: the trapped innocent and the emergence of the trickster. If Latimer's demise can be viewed as Amblerian recognition of the end of innocence and the putative observer, the characters of Carter, Jost, and Brand represent final Amblerian variations on the theme of recrudescence and transformation. The Dionysiac trickster has traveled far "beyond good and evil," and the characters of Carter, Jost, and Brand each suggest an amelioration of the old Dimitrios—but only in degree, not in kind.

Colonels Jost and Brand enter the Dimitrian mentality of antiestablishmentarianism (or, as Lewis calls it, the "giant-killing") when they realize that small individuals and small states are dupes of the conglomerates. As chief intelligence operatives in their countries and now in NATO, they are well aware that the cold war is a pretext that enables the superpowers to conduct business as usual. Brand initiates their extralegal activities of publishing secrets from both superpowers when he tells Jost that they share a common bond of being "instinctive realists." When Jost wants a clarification of the term, Brand smiles broadly and states:

> "A realist in this context," he said, "being one who assumes that most of the secrets we guard so jealously are already well known to the other side, and that most of the secrets the other side guards are already well known to us. One who also understands, however, that the conventions must be observed and the pretences maintained, that outsiders may not look in on our foolishness and that both sides have a common enemy—the small boy who saw that the emperor was naked." (20)

Brand's key word is "instinctive." Following their instinctive urges, Brand and Jost decide to explore their adolescent unconscious and run to the opposites. Professionally, the opposite side is as nefarious as their own—defection to the Eastern bloc is therefore out of the question. Hence, the instinctive urge beckons to Brand, and he finds the alter ego, with the same shadow, in the colleague Jost. Together they discover that the other side of running contrariwise—the *process of enantiodromia*—is not the fatuous exchange of ideologies but the profound exchange of the conscious and unconscious selves. Thus they become the adolescent who tells the world that the emperor is naked. The two wily colonels use the Swiss newsletter known as *Intercom* to broadcast the message of nakedness and vulnerability. And the superpowers are sucked into a bidding for the silence of the anonymous *Intercom.* Jost and Brand retire to their respective dreams and comfort.

Theodore Carter is the major narrative surprise in the novel. First presented through the eyes of Latimer as an alcoholic hack writer, employed as the editor of *Intercom,* Carter is given a depth of character in his developed interiority and moral range of thought. The passages narrated by his loving daughter, Valerie, add a profoundly humanized dimension to his character; this kind of perspective and voice is also employed in *The Levanter,* where Teresa Malandra presents a tender portrait of the human side of Michael Howell.

In an *enantiodromia* of structure, the narrative of the novel runs to the opposite positions of sympathies for the characters of Latimer and Carter. Latimer turns out to be foolish and arrogant; Carter has been mistreated and physically threatened in the takeover of *Intercom.* Carter comes only very slowly to the recognition that he has been publishing explosive superpower secrets in a dangerous game of misinformation and double-cross. In a scene reminiscent of *The Dark Frontier,* Carter crashes his car, loses consciousness, suffers a period of amnesia, and undergoes psychiatric examination. Unlike his ancestor Professor Barstow, however, Carter is capable of transformation and merger with the shadow. He is able to solve the riddle of "the *Intercom* conspiracy," and in a brilliant final scene, he even tracks down the high-living Brand in Majorca. As Wolfe avers: "Carter, the hot-tempered cynic and drunk, has learned to listen. And we listen with him" (174). Carter confronts the dapper and arrogant Brand (who threatens him with a fate like Latimer's) and forces the crafty colonel to tell the truth. Brand, of course, receives assurance that he can continue his good life on the Mediterranean shore.

Wolfe astutely recognizes that the visit to the spy-master is derived from *A Coffin for Dimitrios,* but fails to acknowledge that the torch of illumination is passed from Latimer (and his line of trapped innocents) to Carter (a beneficiary of the Schirmer inheritance). Carter's transformation is noted by the cornered spy-master, Brand. Somewhat akin to the other high priest of the Dionysiac, Phillip Sanger (Ambler's pun, "sane-anger," previously undetected?), Brand "spread out his hands in the gesture of benediction" to the trickster-initiate, Carter:

> You are a different man from the one I met a year ago. Then you were tired and contemptuous of the work you did. You disliked yourself. Now, I detect a new confidence in you. . . . You are engaged in completing a

> book for the late, respected and much lamented Mr. Latimer. . . . You have come to terms with yourself. (207–8)

Like George Carey of *The Schirmer Inheritance,* stopping short of total surrender to the shadow, Theodore Carter bumps into it, and that fleet immersion into that deep well of the self produces a "wellness" that reflects the total conversion of the Schirmers and the Maases. Like all traditional comedy, *The Intercom Conspiracy* ends with a marriage. In this case, Valerie is to be married to the psychiatrist who had examined her father. Like George Carey, who also exits laughing, Theodore Carter is not quite allowed to fully participate in the mysteries, but his existence as witness is regenerative.

Conclusion

The assessment of Eric Ambler's achievement as a popular writer of "spy novels" and fiction of international intrigue must transcend all such parochial labels. Ambler set out to transform these genres of popular literature, but to read his novels is to perceive that the results may not necessarily be what he intended. One senses that Ambler himself entered into a process, much like that of the leitmotif of his best novels, a recurrent motif of radical metamorphosis and rebirth, which drew the Newtonian electrical engineer into a dramatic and unexpected realm of relativity and chaos. In short, Ambler became a purveyor of modernism, and the conveyance happened to be a vehicle much beset and berated by the critics of "received art" and acceptable tastes.

From the perspective of this critique, the critics of the past have done little service to Ambler's reputation by emphasizing the earliest novels so consistently. In paying so much attention to those six prewar novels and at the same time overemphasizing the eleven-year hiatus after the war, the critics have shone a narrow and dim light on a small portion of a sixty-year and eighteen-novel career. With the exception of *A Coffin for Dimitrios,* those celebrated six prewar novels are generally inferior in narrative style and structure than the much more versatile and polysemic novels after the hiatus. *Judgment on Deltchev* and *The Schirmer Inheritance* are crafted by a writer who takes the time to develop character and narrative detail. These two novels reflect an Eric Ambler who did indeed read Nietzsche and Jung, but they exhibit a subtle and considered incorporation of those intellectual influences without the doctrinaire intrusiveness of the prewar novels.

Which is to say, the marvelous transformation of Eric Ambler entails the method and material of his fiction itself. Like one of his "wrong man" protagonists, Ambler is a stilted and stuffy writer of detective/spy novels in the period 1936–41; in 1951, and certainly by 1953, he is a more complex thinker and writer, exploring with tropes of consciousness the terrain of Orwell and Conrad, stylistic light years beyond Somerset Maugham and Graham Greene during that period. Like many of his fictional creations, somewhat trapped and artless, Ambler learns the tricks of the trade. Put another way, the literary trickster delves into the unconscious of his art and devices and emerges as the artist of the metamorphic spy. But the spy is principally the etymological agent of "espionage"—to espy is to witness, and to witness is to know. Eric Ambler takes the figure of the spy—the homeless stranger and distant witness—into the depths of the unconscious and there espies the doppelgänger of the shadow; to witness the "other" within is to know the modern self.

In *The Death and Rebirth of Psychology,* Ira Progoff constructs by way of conclusive arguments a curious correlation that informs the intersection of psychology and metaphysical homelessness in the work of Eric Ambler. Without ever mentioning Ambler, Progoff concludes a lengthy critique of depth psychology by making the earlier "Amblerian" connection between the lessons of depth psychology and the "new physics":

> Depth psychology is in a unique position, for at the point in the foreseeable future when it will finally establish its position as the fundamental science of man, it will do so by validating the very opposite of the materialistic view of life that was the premise of the natural sciences in a day gone by. It will then, in all likelihood, open a psychological road toward the view of the universe emerging from the new physics.
>
> The foundation of the new kind of psychology is its conception of man as an organism of psychological depth and of spiritual magnitude. Its underlying aim is to carry out its psychological work on the unconscious levels of the personality in such a way as to open the dormant potentialities of the spirit and permit them to emerge and unfold.[3]

As the promising young scholarship winner at the University of London, at the callow age of seventeen, Eric Ambler had glimpsed the old and new physics. The distracted and impressionable electrical engineering apprentice found that the conduit to the future lay in the Thames Embankment's courts of law, for there the new physics signaled the profound probings of the new and electric Dionysiac mind and mentality. Precisely as Progoff described it, Ambler instinctively found his own way. Born under the long Victorian shadows of the doomed *Titanic,* Ambler inherited the twentieth century's compelling task of deconstructing the old, eighteenth-century myth of the "perfectibility of the human." The new physics and the return of the Nietzschean and Jungian encounter with the shadow of the ancient and distant self became a new intellectual battleground. Ambler perceived the spiritual homesickness of the conscious self for its unconscious other—and the dangers akin to that metaphysical reunion.

Eric Ambler's stateless and alienated protagonists capture for a popular literary audience the twentieth-century obsession with metaphysical homelessness. The self-absorbed critique of the epoch's spiritual rootlessness was defined early in the century by the investigations of depth psychology. One of Ambler's definitive contributions to the genres of popular and suspense fiction entails the interpenetrations of the consciousness of the popular reading audience and followers of Freud's and Jung's explorations of the modern mind and its "scientific" structures. In some ways, perhaps, the theorists of the dynamics of a modern popular culture might even argue that the immediate and sustained (never fully intended) popular interest in arcane and academic investigations into newly discovered "altered states of consciousness" influentially shaped the course and contents of Anglo-American popular culture. And, of course, that this modern science should arise at the same time that the twentieth-century enigma—Nazi Germany in all of its cultured and brutal glory—should rear up before the Western world, was either pure happenstance or incontrovertible proof of Jungian synchronicity. Ambler's use of Nazi Germany to reflect the both horrendous and ebullient outbreak of the modern Dionysiac spirit was a literary and psychological coup of brilliant proportions. Ambler read clearly the interior contours of the Western world.

After the threat of the Jungian "blond beast" had been quelled in 1945, Ambler by self-admission had to reexplore those interior contours. And at this juncture, he experienced his second major transformation as a writer as he explored the sustained and sharply critical themes of decolonization and Orientalism. Ambler carried his prewar condemnations of "big business and war" to a postwar world of political independence movements, adding an Orwellian squint on empire and ethnocentrism. Consistently drawn to the East by his search for the origins of Dionysiac mysteries and power, Ambler inevitably arrived at the Orient. Throughout the five Oriental novels, as described in chapter 6, Ambler's two great themes of the power of the unconscious and the mystery of the East coalesced; in the transformation of the trickster hero, the original Dimitrios, into the Franz Schirmers and the Piet Maases, Ambler found an ameliorated Dionysus who came to represent the modern portrait of the individuated self. That delineation of the balanced, modern self foregrounded the trickster's ability to change and adapt according to the mutable conditions of the environment—all the while attuned to the shifting forces of the Apollonian conscious self and the Dionysiac shadow.

In his critique of Western bias toward the East, characterized by Said's use of the ethnocentric term "Orientalism," Ambler came to illustrate the bifurcated psyche of the modern human being in his portraits of the so-called "mongrel"; his theme of miscegenation and the disenfranchised progeny of those relationships recurs throughout the five Oriental novels. The label preferred in this critique has been "the double-heritaged hero." Ambler's sympathetic depiction of these doubly endowed characters is the first in a popular genre traditionally etched by a deep and abiding ethnocentrism.

In many ways, Ambler's novels belong to another popular genre—that of travel writing—which has been insightfully described by Paul Fussell in *Abroad: British Literary Traveling between the Wars.*[4] Fussell claims that the 1920s and 1930s were the final age of literary traveling, when the independent traveler—almost always the scion of colonial design, became an endangered species. This traveler, an unmistakable envoy of empire, was nearly always European or North American, middle- or upper-class, and a white male. This figure would roam the world in search of adventure, discovery, knowledge, redemption, or disillusionment—all of which were abstracted from utopian idylls and converted into the molding of a better character for return to the dystopian domains of civilization. Fussell's critical study has been extended in the 1992 publication of Mary Louise Pratt's *Imperial Eyes.*[5] Pratt's intention is to demystify the experience of the Western traveler. She argues that this experience was immune to the political and economic influences that shaped the colonial development of places such as Latin America and Africa. She grounds these travelogues in the complex web of Western rationalizations of an ambivalent and often violent history of capitalist and imperial expansion.

Needless to say, Conrad and Orwell were the vanguard of the reactionary and liberal challenge during the proletarian 1930s to this popular but complicit genre. Ambler, whose instincts in both political and philosophical terms were rooted in that same decade and its ideology, was instrumental in transforming the popular novel of international intrigue by introducing such radical elements as miscegenation, dual-heritaged protagonists, and the elementary dignity of "decolonized" peoples. Even in *The Levanter,* where Ambler exposes the vicious agenda of terrorism, the agonizing dilemma of the Palestinian homeland is depicted without Middle Eastern stereotypes. Michael Howell is doubly endowed by both East and West; Ambler attempts to find the mediated middle, whether it is the conflicted human psyche or the tormented lands of the ancient Near East. Both Apollo and Dionysus constitute the wholeness of humanity and its multiplicity of cultures.

Ambler's developmental explorations of the "spy novel" and the literature of international intrigue, particularly in the materials and methods of his novels of the 1950s, blazed the trail for the accomplished innovations of John Le Carré, which reflect Ambler's great themes of the unconscious other and the universality of the conflicted human mind and its myriad of cultures. Le Carré's *Looking Glass War* has as its central metaphor the gaze of the distant and alienated observer; the nature of that gaze that would articulate the "other" as forever alien. But Ambler, and later Le Carré, turn those transformative and appropriative "Western eyes" into the looking glass's apprehension of the sameness of the observer and the other. Ambler's most memorable coup was to take a genre that marginalized and distanced the "others" of the colonized lands of the British Empire and to transform that literature into a looking glass that examined the self and found the alter ego.

Notes and References

The first reference to each source is listed in the notes; subsequent references are cited parenthetically in the text.

Preface

1. Eric Ambler, "Introduction," *The Dark Frontier* (New York: Mysterious Press, 1991), xvi.

2. Gavin Lambert, *The Dangerous Edge* (New York: Grossman, 1975), 108.

Chapter One

1. Joel Hopkins, "An Interview with Eric Ambler," *Journal of Popular Culture* 9 (1975): 286.

2. Jacob Bronowski, *Science and Human Values* (New York: J. Messner, 1945).

3. On Jung's "condensation": In the notion of condensation, as Jung applied it to the collective unconscious, is the historical dimension to the unconscious. In short, Jung concluded that the background of the psyche included not only personal data but also the historical layerings of data common to all human beings. The individual psyche contained both ontogenetic and phylogenetic records.

On Jung's "transfer": The source of energy in the Jungian apparatus of depth psychology is libido. "Libido" is the natural energy that serves the basic life drives; however, that energy in excess of instinctive ends can be converted (or transferred) to productive and more socialized (cultural) purposes. Transfer is the mechanism whereby a symbol is produced that can direct the libido into the conduit away from the instinctive and toward the productive, socialized, and cultural. The symbol is never consciously evoked, but rather is delivered as intuition or in dreamworks.

4. Eric Ambler, *Here Lies: An Autobiography* (New York: Mysterious Press, 1988), 22.

5. Elleston Trevor, "Introduction," *A Coffin for Dimitrios* (Del Mar: University of California Press, 1977), vii–viii.

6. Julian Symons, *Mortal Consequences: A History from the Detective Story to the Crime Novel* (New York: Harper and Row, 1972), 238.

7. Hugh Eames, *Sleuths, Inc.* (Philadelphia: Lippincott Co., 1978), 150.

8. John Cawelti and Bruce Rosenberg, *The Spy Story* (Chicago: University of Chicago Press, 1987), 109.

9. Quoted in *Contemporary Authors,* New Revision Series, vol. 7 (Detroit: Gale Research Co., 1984), 23.10.

10. Eric Ambler, "Introduction," *Waiting for Orders* (New York: Mysterious Press, 1991), 2.

11. The chronology of the history of *The Light of Day* was found in Ambler's collected papers, Special Collections, Mugar Library, Boston University.

Chapter Two

1. For an interesting discussion of the detective, see Elliot G. Gilbert, "The Detective as Metaphor in the Nineteenth Century," *Journal of Popular Culture* 1 (Winter 1967): 256–62.

2. Donald A. Ringe, *James Fenimore Cooper* (New Haven, Conn.: College and University Press, 1962), 28.

3. Lionel Trilling, "*The Princess Casamassima,*" in *The Liberal Imagination* (New York: Doubleday, 1940), 65.

4. Letter to Louise Crombie Ambler, 22 December 1940, from the Ambler collected papers. Quoted by permission of Mugar Library, Boston University.

5. Eric Ambler, ed., "Introduction," *To Catch a Spy: An Anthology of Favorite Spy Stories* (New York: Bantam Books, 1966), 9.

6. Morton Dauwen Zabel, "Introduction," *Under Western Eyes* by Joseph Conrad (New York: Doubleday and Co., 1951), xvii.

7. Joseph Conrad, *The Secret Agent* (New York: Doubleday Anchor Books, 1953), 67–68.

8. R. W. Stallman, "Time and *The Secret Agent,*" *Texas Studies in Literature and Language* 1 (Spring 1959): 122.

9. Graham Greene, "The Last Buchan," in *The Lost Childhood* (New York: Viking Press, 1966), 104.

10. Eric Ambler, *Journey into Fear* (New York: Bantam, 1972), 17.

11. Eric Ambler, *A Coffin for Dimitrios* (New York: Bantam, 1972), 174–75; in-text citations are from this edition.

Chapter Three

1. C. G. Jung, *Collected Papers on Analytical Psychology* (New York: Moffat Yard and Co., 1917), 1–2.

2. James Moore, *Gurdjieff* (Rockport, Mass.: Element, 1991), in a lengthy footnote on p. 342, discusses Gurdjieff's contribution to the development of experimental psychology:

> It was William James (1842–1910) who offered the dictum "my experience is what I agree to attend to," but it was Gurdjieff who extrapolated

this insight into a *pratique* for the mobilization and direction of attention, within the context of a persuasive phenomenology of consciousness. By the last decade of the twentieth century the various proponents of gestalt, transactional psychology, S-R learning theory, the Jungians, the Kleinians, and embattled Freudians, had long since consigned attention to the ideological and methodological periphery, leaving only lay Gurdjieffians working on attention, according to their canon, as the quintessential challenge to understanding. For a succinct evocation of the Gurdjieffian position, see William Segal, "The Force of Attention," *The Structure of Man,* Green River Press, Stillgate Publishers, Vermont, 1987.

3. Shepherd Ivory Franz, *Persons One and Three* (London: Whittlesey House, McGraw-Hill Book Co., 1933).

4. Anonymous, *I Lost My Memory: The Case as the Patient Saw It* (London: Faber and Faber, 1932), 78–80.

5. Interestingly enough, in *I Lost My Memory,* the patient loses his memory in mid-April; Barstow cannot account for a period from 17 April to 26 May.

6. C. G. Jung, *Two Essays on Analytical Psychology* (New York: Meridian Books, 1956), 155. Note that although Ambler used the *Collected Papers* (1917), I have used more recent editions, such as this 1956 *Two Essays.*

7. William Barrett, *Irrational Man* (New York: Anchor, 1962), 177–93.

8. David Lehman, "Epitaph for a Spymaster," *Partisan Review* 54 (Spring 1987): 334.

9. Eric Ambler, *Background to Danger* (New York: Alfred A. Knopf, 1937), 111.

10. Irving Howe, ed., "Introduction," *New Grub Street* (Boston: Houghton Mifflin, 1962), xii–xiii.

11. See chapter 1, note 3, for brief explanations of Jung's concepts of condensation and transfer.

12. Eric Ambler, *Epitaph for a Spy* (New York: Alfred A. Knopf, 1952), 3.

13. Eric Ambler, *Cause for Alarm* (New York: Bantam Books, 1974), 105.

14. M. Silk and J. Stern, *Nietzsche on Tragedy* (Cambridge: Cambridge University Press, 1981), 34–36.

15. Bernard Bergonzi, *The Myth of Modernism and Twentieth Century Literature* (New York: St. Martin's Press, 1986), 124.

Chapter Four

1. Ambler's preference for Jung is stated in the introduction to the 1991 edition of *The Dark Frontier.*

2. Because Ambler himself first used the title *A Coffin for Dimitrios,* I will use his and Knopf's preference.

3. Julian Symons, "An End to Spying, or From Pipe Dream to Farce," *Times Literary Supplement,* 12 December 1968, 1411–12.

4. Friedrich Nietzsche, *The Philosophy of Nietzsche* (New York: Modern Library, 1954), 428–29.

5. One is tempted to cite Nicholas Meyer's best-selling 1976 novel, *The Seven Percent Solution,* as a recent example of the same linkage—the novel of detection that explores physical and psychic evidence. Sherlock Holmes is joined in this contemporary novel by Freud, not Jung.

6. C. G. Jung, *Symbols of Transformation* (Princeton, N.J.: Princeton University Press, 1967), 337n, 415n.

7. Oswald Spengler, *The Decline of the West* (New York: Oxford University Press, 1991), 3.

8. See Jung's *Man and His Symbols* (New York: Dell Publishing Co., 1968).

9. V. Walter Odajnyk, *Jung and Politics* (New York: New York University Press, 1976). See chapter 6, "The German Case."

Chapter Five

1. Even the American novel *To Kill a Mockingbird* is actually a trial story that examines old war crimes of ethnic hatreds and racism, a legacy of the Civil War and earlier times.

2. In Oswald Spengler's last published work, *The Hour of Decision* (1934), he discusses topics such as "the white economic system already undermined by 1900" and the threat of the coming "coloured world-revolution." Spengler calls for the German national spirit to reawaken.

3. Peter Lewis, *Eric Ambler* (New York: Continuum, 1990), 90–91. Note that Lewis argues well for the theory that Albania is the model state for "Ixania," the country named in Ambler's first novel and, presumably, though unnamed, the country that is trying Deltchev in this novel. Although both Albania and Bulgaria seem to fit the model, I would present the case for Bulgaria. Note that Bulgaria figures prominently in *A Coffin for Dimitrios;* this tends to show Ambler's continued knowledge of and fascination with it.

4. Eric Ambler, *Judgment on Deltchev* (New York: Carrol and Graf, 1991), 5.

5. Additionally, it would seem that the trial of Yordan Deltchev is based on the actual 1948 trial and execution of Traichko Kostov, a Bulgarian "national" communist. In the same year, Bulgaria joined COMECON (a Communist economic bloc from the Cold War period), and later the Warsaw Pact.

6. Eric Ambler, *The Schirmer Inheritance* (New York: Carroll and Graf, 1991), 2.

7. Joseph Campbell, "Editor's Introduction," *The Portable Jung* (New York: Viking Press, 1971), xxvi.

8. Thomas Belmonte, "The Trickster and the Sacred Clown, Revealing the Logic of the Un-speakable," in *C. G. Jung and the Humanities: Towards a Hermeneutics of Culture,* ed. Karin Barnaby and P. D'Acierno (Princeton, N.J.: Princeton University Press, 1990), 52.

Chapter Six

1. Edward W. Said, *Orientalism* (New York: Pantheon Books, 1978), 57.
2. Eric Ambler, *State of Siege* (New York: Bantam Books, 1957), 1.
3. Peter Wolfe, *Alarms and Epitaphs: The Art of Eric Ambler* (Bowling Green, Ohio: Popular Press, 1993), 102.
4. Eric Ambler, *Passage of Arms* (New York: Ballantine Books, 1977), 1.
5. Eric Ambler, *The Light of Day* (Kingswood, Surrey: Reprint Society of London, 1964), 6.
6. Eric Ambler, *Dirty Story: A Further Account of the Life and Adventures of Arthur Abdel Simpson* (New York: Atheneum, 1967), 11.
7. Eric Ambler, *The Levanter* (New York: Atheneum, 1972), 28.

Chapter Seven

1. Eric Ambler, *A Kind of Anger* (New York: Bantam, 1964), 43.
2. Eric Ambler, *The Intercom Conspiracy* (New York: Atheneum, 1969), 22–23.
3. Ira Progroff, *The Death and Rebirth of Psychology* (New York: Dell, 1964), 264–65.
4. Paul Fussell, *Abroad: British Literary Traveling between the Wars* (New York: Oxford University Press, 1980).
5. Mary Louise Pratt, *Imperial Eyes* (London: Routledge, 1992).

Selected Bibliography

PRIMARY WORKS

Novels

The Dark Frontier. London: Hodder and Stoughton, 1936.

Uncommon Danger. London: Hodder and Stoughton, 1937. Rpt. as *Background to Danger.* New York: Alfred A. Knopf, 1937.

Epitaph for a Spy. London: Hodder and Stoughton. 1938. Rev. version. New York: Alfred A. Knopf, 1952.

Cause for Alarm. London: Hodder and Stoughton, 1938. New York: Alfred A. Knopf, 1939.

The Mask of Dimitrios. London: Hodder and Stoughton, 1939. Rpt. as *A Coffin for Dimitrios.* New York: Alfred A. Knopf, 1939.

Journey into Fear. London: Hodder and Stoughton, 1940. New York: Alfred A. Knopf, 1940.

Judgment on Deltchev. London: Hodder and Stoughton, 1951. New York: Alfred A. Knopf, 1951.

The Schirmer Inheritance. London: Heinemann, 1953. New York: Alfred A. Knopf, 1953.

The Night-Comers. London: Heinemann, 1956. Rpt. as *State of Siege.* New York: Alfred A. Knopf, 1956.

Passage of Arms. London: Heinemann, 1959. New York: Alfred A. Knopf, 1960.

The Light of Day. London: Heinemann, 1962. New York: Alfred A. Knopf, 1963. Rpt. as *Topkapi.* New York: Bantam, 1964.

A Kind of Anger. London: Bodley Head, 1964. New York: Atheneum, 1964.

Dirty Story: A Further Account of the Life and Adventures of Arthur Abdel Simpson. London: Bodley Hill, 1967. New York: Atheneum, 1967.

The Intercom Conspiracy. New York: Atheneum, 1969. London: Weidenfeld and Nicolson, 1970. Rpt. as *A Quiet Conspiracy.* Glasgow: Fontana/Collins, 1989.

The Levanter. London: Weidenfeld and Nicolson, 1972. New York: Atheneum, 1972.

Doctor Frigo. London: Weidenfeld and Nicolson, 1974. New York: Atheneum, 1974.

Send No More Roses. London: Weidenfeld and Nicolson, 1977. Rpt. as *The Siege of the Villa Lipp.* New York: Random House, 1977.

The Care of Time. London: Weidenfeld and Nicolson, 1981. New York: Farrar, Straus and Giroux, 1981.

Other Books

The Ability to Kill and Other Pieces. London: Bodley Head, 1963. Rpt. as *The Ability to Kill: True Tales of Bloody Murder.* New York and London: Mysterious Press, 1987.

To Catch a Spy: An Anthology of Favorite Spy Stories. Edited by Eric Ambler. London: Bodley Head, 1964. New York: Atheneum, 1965.

Here Lies: An Autobiography. London: Weidenfeld and Nicolson, 1985. New York: Farrar, Straus, and Giroux, 1986.

Short Stories

"The Army of the Shadows." In *The Queen's Book of the Red Cross,* edited by Vincent Starrett. London: Hodder and Stoughton, 1939. Rpt. as *World's Greatest Spy Stories.* Cleveland: World, 1944, 46–61.

"Belgrade 1926." In *To Catch a Spy,* 156–80.

"The Blood Bargain." In *Winter's Crimes 2,* edited by George Hardinge, 9–26. London: Macmillan, 1970. *Ellery Queen's Windows of Mystery,* edited by Ellery Queen. New York: Dial, 1980. See also *The Best of Winter's Crimes,* edited by George Hardinge. London: Macmillan, 1986. And see *The Mammoth Book of Modern Crime Stories,* edited by George Hardinge. London: Robinson, 1987.

"The Case of the Pinchbeck Locket." (London) *Sketch,* 3 July 1940, 24–26. *Ellery Queen's Mystery Magazine* 6, no. 25 (November 1945): 97–101. *Best Mystery Stories,* edited by Maurice Richardson, 157–68. London: Faber, 1948.

"The Case of the Emerald Sky." *Sketch,* 10 July 1940, 191. *EQMM* 6, no. 21 (March 1945): 38–45. *To the Queen's Taste,* edited by Ellery Queen, 281–90. Boston: Little, Brown, 1946. See also *The Arbor House Treasury of Mystery and Suspense,* edited by Bill Pronzini, Barry H. Malzberg, and Martin H. Greenberg. New York: Arbor House, 1981.

"The Case of the Cycling Chauffeur." *Sketch,* 17 July 1940, 88, 90. Rpt. as "A Bird in the Tree." *EQMM* 9, no. 42 (May 1947): 42–47.

"The Case of the Overheated Service Flat." *Sketch,* 24 July 1940, 120, 122. Rpt. as "Case of the Overheated Flat." *EQMM* 11, no. 53 (April 1948): 35–39.

"The Case of the Drunken Socrates." *Sketch,* 31 July 1940, 150, 152. Rpt. as "Case of the Landlady's Brother." *EQMM* 13, no. 63 (February 1949): 121–25. *Best Mystery Stories,* edited by Maurice Richardson, 169–78. London: Faber, 1948.

"The Case of the Gentleman Poet." *Sketch,* 7 August 1940, 186, 188. Rpt. as "The Case of the Gentleman Poet." *EQMM* 10, no. 46 (September 1947): 76–83.

Waiting for Orders: The Complete Short Stories of Eric Ambler. New York: Mysterious Press, 1991.

Screenplays

The Way Ahead. 1944. With Peter Ustinov.
The October Man. 1946.
The Passionate Friends. 1948. (From the novel by H. G. Wells.)
Highly Dangerous. 1950.
The Magic Box. 1951. (From a biography of W. Friese-Greene.)
Campbell's Kingdom. 1952
The Card. 1952. (From the novel by Arnold Bennett.)
Gigolo and Gigolette. 1952. (From a short story by W. Somerset Maugham.)
Rough Shoot. 1952. (From the novel by Geoffrey Household.)
The Cruel Sea. 1953. (From the novel by Nicholas Monsarrat.)
The Purple Plain. 1953. (From a novel by H. E. Bates.)
Lease of Life. 1954. (From a story by Patrick Jenjins.)
Windom's Way. 1954.
Body Below. 1955.
Nightrunners of Bengal. 1955.
The Yangtse Incident. 1956.
The Guns of Navarone. 1957.
The Night-Comers. 1957.
A Night to Remember. 1957. (From the book by Walter Lord.)
Blind Date. 1958.
The Eye of Truth. 1958.
The Wreck of the Mary Deare. 1959. (From the novel by Hammond Innes.)
Love Hate Love. 1970.

The "Eliot Reed" Novels

Skytip. Garden City, N.Y.: Doubleday, 1950; London: Hodder and Stoughton, 1951.
Tender to Danger. Garden City, N.Y.: Doubleday, 1951. Rpt. as *As Tender to Moonlight.* London: Hodder and Stoughton, 1952.
The Maras Affair. Garden City, N.Y.: Doubleday, 1953; London: Collins, 1953.
Charter to Danger. London: Collins, 1954.
Passport to Panic. London: Collins, 1958.

Uncollected Essays

"The Novelist and Films." In *Crime in Good Company: Essays on Criminals and Crime-Writing,* edited by Michael Gilbert, 192–209. Boston: The Writer, 1959.
"Introduction." In *The Adventures of Sherlock Holmes,* 7–11. London: John Murray and Jonathan Cape, 1974.
"A Better Sort of Rubbish: An Inquiry into the State of the Thriller." *Times Saturday Review,* 30 November 1974, 8.

"The End of the Affair." *New Statesman,* 13 January 1978, 56.

"Voyages and Shipwrecks." In *Whodunit? A Guide to Crime, Suspense, and Spy Fiction,* edited by H. R. F. Keating, 104–7. London: Windward, 1982; New York: Van Nostrand Reinhold, 1982.

Archival Material

The Eric Ambler Archive. Special Collections Department, Mugar Memorial Library, Boston University.

SECONDARY WORKS

Criticism and Commentary

Adams, Phoebe. "This Trade of Gunrunning." *Atlantic,* April 1960, 114.

Ambrosetti, Ronald. "The World of Eric Ambler: From Detective to Spy." In *Dimensions of Detective Fiction,* edited by Larry N. Landrum, Pat Browne, and Ray B. Browne, 102–9. Bowling Green, Ohio: Bowling Green State University Popular Press, 1976.

Amory, Mark. "The Ambler Way." *Sunday Times Magazine,* 5 January 1975, 30–32.

Anderson, Isaac. "A Spy Story." *New York Times Book Review,* 29 January 1939, 7.

Barzun, Jacques, and Wendell Hertig Taylor. *A Catalogue of Crime.* New York: Harper and Row, 1971.

Bayley, John. "Madly Excited." *London Review of Books,* 1 June 1989, 3, 5.

Bergonzi, Bernard. *The Myth of Modernism and Twentieth Century Literature.* New York: St. Martin's Press, 1986.

Boucher, Anthony. "Trouble in Sunda." *New York Times Book Review.* 23 September 1956, 31.

Brinton, Crane. *Nietzsche.* New York: Harper and Row, 1965.

Buckley, Priscilla L. "Of Banana Republics and Habsborgs." *National Review,* 20 December 1974, 1475.

Cain, James M. "Color of the East." *New York Times Book Review,* 6 March 1960, 38.

Campbell, Joseph, ed. *The Portable Jung.* New York: Penguin, 1971.

Cawelti, John G., and Bruce A. Rosenberg. *The Spy Story.* Chicago: University of Chicago Press, 1987, 101–14.

"Confidential Agents." *Times Literary Supplement,* 20 July 1956, 434.

Davis, Dorothy Salisbury. "Some of the Truth." *Colloquium on Crime: Eleven Renowned Mystery Writers Discuss Their Work,* edited by Robin Winks, 63–78. New York: Scribners, 1986.

Davis, Paxton. "The World We Live In: The Novels of Eric Ambler." *Hollins Critic* 8 (February 1971): 1–11.

Day Lewis, Cecil. "With a Flair for Creating Alarm." *New York Times Book Review,* 26 July 1953, 5.

Demarest, Michael. "Forever Ambler." *Time,* 14 September 1981, 98.

Du Bois, William. "Journey into Terror." *New York Times Book Review,* 18 March 1951, 5.

Eames, Hugh. *Sleuths, Inc.* Philadelphia: Lippincott, 1978.

Elliott, Charles. "Ambling On." *Time,* 26 June 1972, 92–93.

Fenton, James. "The Ambler Memorandum." *Vogue* (United Kingdom), July 1977, 100–102.

Frazer, Sir James George. *The New Golden Bough,* edited by Theodor Gaster. New York: Criterion, 1959.

Fuller, Roy. "Warts and All." *TLS,* 22 November 1974, 1307.

Gilbert, Michael. "The Professionals and the Predatory Pikes." *TLS,* 5 June 1981, 626.

Ginna, Robert Emmett. "Bio: Outside His Window, within His Heart, Eric Ambler Finds the Stuff of Great Spy Novels." *People,* 6 June 1977, 92–95, 100.

Gray, Paul. "Capital Gains." *Time,* 6 June 1977, 97.

Greene, Graham. "The Sense of Apprehension." *Month,* July 1951, 49–51.

Grella, George. "Who's for Treachery." *New York Times Book Review,* 8 October 1967.

Haycraft, Howard. "Introduction." *Five Spy Novels, Selected and Introduced by Howard Haycraft.* Garden City, N.Y.: Doubleday, c. 1962.

Heald, Tim. "Chilled Vintage Old Ambler." *Times,* 13 June 1985.

Hillerman, Tony. "Mystery, Country Boys, and the Big Reservation." *Colloquium on Crime: Eleven Renowned Mystery Writers Discuss Their Work,* edited by Robin Winks, 127–47. New York: Scribners, 1986.

Hitchcock, Alfred. "Introduction." *Intrigue: The Great Spy Novels of Eric Ambler.* New York: Alfred A. Knopf, 1943, vii–xi.

Hogan, William. "Eric Ambler Covers a Coup in the Indies." *San Francisco Chronicle,* 1 October 1956, 25.

Hopkins, Joel. "An Interview with Eric Ambler." *Journal of Popular Culture* 9 (Fall 1975): 285–93.

Hubin, Allen J. "The Intercom Conspiracy." *New York Times Book Review,* 21 September 1969, 44.

James, Clive. "Prisoners of Clarity-2: Eric Ambler." *New Review,* September 1974, 63–69.

Jung, Carl Gustav. *Collected Papers on Analytical Psychology.* New York: Moffat Yard and Co., 1917.

_____. *Symbols of Transformation.* Princeton, N.J.: Princeton University Press, 1967.

_____. *Two Essays on Analytical Psychology.* New York: Meridian Books, 1953.

Kauffmann, Stanley. "Simple Simenon." *New Republic,* 9 December 1967, 24, 38.

Kominis, Katherine. "Heroes among Us: Eric Ambler's Novels of Intrigue." *Firsts*, June 1993, 24–29.

Krim, Seymour. "Suspense." *Commonweal,* 7 August 1953, 450–51.

Krutch, Joseph Wood. "Mr. Ambler's Spies." *New York Times Book Review,* 16 March 1952, 4.

Lambert, Gavin. *The Dangerous Edge.* New York: Grossman, 1976, 104–31.

Lehman, David. "Epitaph for a Spymaster." *Partisan Review,* Spring 1987, 334–38.

Lewis, Peter. *Eric Ambler.* New York: Continuum, 1990.

Mitgang, Herbert. "Interview: The Thrilling Eric Ambler." *New York Times Book Review,* 13 September 1981, 3, 22, 24.

Moore, James. *Gurdjieff.* Rockport, Mass.: Element Books, 1991.

"Mystery and Crime." *New Yorker,* 2 March 1963, 152.

New York Herald Tribune Book Review, 15 April 1951, 15.

Odajnyk, Volodymyr Walter. *Jung and Politics.* New York: New York University Press, 1976.

Offord, Lenore Glen. "Melodrama in Sumatra in the Ambler Manner." In "This Week," *San Francisco Chronicle,* 27 March 1960, 25.

Oram, Malcolm. "Eric Ambler." *Publishers Weekly,* 9 September 1974, 6, 7.

Otto, Warren F. *Dionysus: Myth and Cult.* Bloomington: Indiana University Press, 1965.

Panek, Le Roy L. *The Special Branch: The British Spy Story, 1890–1980.* Bowling Green, Ohio: Bowling Green State University Popular Press, 1981, 138–54.

Prescott, Peter S. "I Spy." *Newsweek,* 14 October 1974, 125–26.

Progoff, Ira. *The Death and Rebirth of Psychology.* New York: Dell Publishing Co., 1964.

Reilly, John M., ed. *Twentieth-Century Crime and Mystery Writers.* 2d ed. New York: St. Martin's Press, 1985.

"Return to the Balkans." *Time,* 19 March 1951, 118.

Russell, John. "Summer Reading: Art." *New York Times Book Review,* 31 May 1987, 11.

Said, Edward W. *Orientalism.* New York: Pantheon Books, 1978.

Scott, J. D. "New Novels." *New Statesman and Nation,* 25 August 1951, 211.

Spengler, Oswald. *The Decline of the West.* Abridged ed. With an introduction by H. Stuart Hughes. New York: Oxford University Press, 1991.

Steinbrunner, Chris, and Otto Penzler, eds. *Encyclopedia of Mystery and Detection.* New York: McGraw-Hill, 1976, 7–9.

"Subtleties of Power." *New York Times Book Review,* 13 September 1981, 3, 24, 26.

Symons, Julian. *Mortal Consequences: A History from the Detective Story to the Crime Novel.* New York: Harper and Row, 1972.

Taylor, David. "Passing Through: Eric Ambler Talks to David Taylor." *Punch,* 6 September 1972, 310.

Wegmann, Karl Heinz. "Filmographic Eric Ambler." *Filmkritik* 26, no. 12 (December 1982): 595–99.

Young, Stanley. "Intrigue, 1937 Style." *New York Times Book Review,* 8 August 1937, 37.

Unpublished Master's Thesis

Linville, Karen Marie. "The Film Adaptations of the Detective and Spy Novels of Dashiell Hammett, Raymond Chandler, and Eric Ambler." UCLA, Theater Arts, 1974. Filmography included.

Index

The Author

Ronald J. Ambrosetti is professor of English and associate dean of arts and sciences at State University of New York College at Fredonia. He holds an M.A. and a Ph.D. from Bowling Green State University and an A.B. from Loyola College in Baltimore.

He is coeditor with Ray B. Browne of two anthologies, *Continuities in Popular Culture* and *Popular Culture and Curricula,* and has published numerous articles in the areas of American literature, folklore and popular culture in *Keystone Folklore,* in the *Journal of the American Studies Association of Texas,* and in the *Journal of American Culture.*

He was a Fulbright lecturer in American studies in Coimbra, Portugal, and corecipient of a grant from the Department of Health, Education and Welfare for ethnic heritage studies. He has also worked as a speech writer and curriculum specialist for the Office of the Army Surgeon General and served on active duty with the U.S. Army.